100 TIMES

100

TIMES

A MEMOIR OF SEXISM

CHAVISA WOODS

SEVEN STORIES PRESS

new york • oakland • london

Seven Stories Press
140 Watts Street
New York, NY 10013
www.sevenstories.com

College professors and high school and middle school teachers can order free examination copies of Seven Stories Press titles. To order, visit www.sevenstories.com, or send fax on school letterhead to 212-226-1411.

Library of Congress Cataloging-in-Publication Data

Names: Woods, Chavisa, author.
Title: 100 times : a memoir of sexism / Chavisa Woods.
Other titles: A hundred times
Description: First Edition. | New York : Seven Stories Press, 2019.
Identifiers: LCCN 2019003613| ISBN 9781609809133 (paperback) | ISBN 9781609809140 (ebook)
Subjects: LCSH: Woods, Chavisa. | Rape--United States--Case studies. | Victims--United States--Case studies. | Sex crimes z United States--Case studies. | Sexism--United States--Case studies. | BISAC: BIOGRAPHY & AUTOBIOGRAPHY / Women.
Classification: LCC HV6561 .W66 2019 | DDC 362.88092/520973--dc23
LC record available at https://lccn.loc.gov/2019003613

Printed in the USA.

9 8 7 6 5 4 3 2 1

preface

In this book, I've cataloged one hundred formative incidents of sexist discrimination, violence, sexual harassment, assault, and attempted rape I've experienced from childhood to now, to paint a clear picture of the impact sexism has had on me throughout my life.

All my life when I've tried to talk to men about sexism, my main obstacle has been trying to convince them, quite simply, that it exists.

I've exhausted myself trying to get men to understand that sexism is something that actually has a critical and near-constant impact on my life. When I'm trying to convey this to a man who is questioning me, I usually start by telling a story; often, one of the stories I've included in this book. I recount an instance of sexual assault or harassment in detail. Many men then counter these narratives by telling me about one time when a woman smacked their ass at a bar, or made an overt come-on to them. But, these men tell me, they didn't mind it. The implication being, I am overreacting to an incident that has an equivalent in the lives of men.

But I'm not just talking about things I didn't mind or things that were invited, and I'm not talking about one or two times. I'm not talking about ten or twenty times. I'm talking about at least *one hundred* times. Actually, many more.

When I talk to most women about these things (and we

do talk about it often with each other), there is an immediate understanding that the sexist incidents are part of an endless stream of experiences we've learned to endure as a built-in aspect of female life.

I struggled to write this introduction. I asked friends and fellow writers what they thought I needed to cover in the introduction, and I had a list of topics I wanted to be sure to clarify.

I was told that I should give some sort of warning, or note that if you are someone who has experienced multiple, brutal incidents of sexual assault, harassment, violence, and discrimination, maybe you shouldn't read this book in one sitting. I do not shy away from clear and sometimes graphic descriptions of the things that I've experienced and witnessed. This includes homophobic, sexist, and racist slurs, among other forms of verbal violence. I was asked what I hope women who are already aware of the sexism we face every day would get out of reading this book. I do hope that there is value in hearing another woman's story, and in knowing that you are not alone in your experience.

I was having difficulty contextualizing everything I wanted to convey. I wanted to be sure to talk about why I haven't named any men who harassed or assaulted me in this book. I've left many of these descriptions quite anonymous, actually. I've done this partly because I believe that public persecution and punishment of individuals has huge limitations when speaking of changing a larger, systemic social issue, and I have seen that *all* men have been socialized to participate in sexist behavior. Though there are a handful of men described in this book who *are* serial sexual predators, and who I *have* named within my community, and to people who need to know that they are dangerous, none of these men (who are serial sexual predators) are particularly powerful or famous, so, in the context of this book, naming them would only be sensational.

I wanted to tell the reader that, while it may seem odd, a few of the men described in this book are still dear to me. I don't necessarily think of every man who has hurt me with sexism as a monster. And I think that is something specific to sexism. Most women have lived with a dyadic relationship with men all of our lives. We've always known that even the men we love the most view us, and often treat women in general, as something "other," something less than. This has to change. I have been waiting for it to change all of my life. And now, I am demanding it. I may still love some of the men who have treated me in sexist ways, but the way women have been treated for all of human history, and even to this day, is unconscionable, and unforgivable.

I wanted to be sure to clarify that I know that all women have to deal with sexism from the time they are born or come out as/transition to being women. I wanted to make sure I made clear that trans women, queer women, and straight cis women alike have to bear the burden of sexism.

Above all this, there was something else I wanted to weave in, something that always evaded me when I searched for words to describe it. I began writing about the feminist texts I've read that have granted lucidity to my journey toward awareness of how my experience as a human has been defined by the fact that I'm a woman. I've struggled to find the ability to name the murky obstacles on my craggy path, which have remained invisible to so many, it seems, because they are as intermingled into our existence as water particles in misty air. It is difficult to realize that the precipices you are attempting to surmount aren't what cause you to slip. Rather, the condition of the atmosphere itself is to blame for the slickness that disallows achieving a certain foothold.

What is this atmosphere, though? What is this thing? I believed it had something to do with a conceit of ownership of all women, by men, couched in a camouflage of supposed intimacy. It was hard to put into words, but it seemed to have something to do with old tropes like the yin and yang, of some assumed harmony between men and women, where each has a certain role, which translates into a feeling of individual women owing all individual men something, a certain type of sweetness, affection, and intimacy, which is so often used as a means for individual men to invade and control individual women in countless ways.

I was struggling to eke this out, so I picked up a book by one of my favorite feminist writers, hoping it would jog something in my mind; get me writing on a good track again. The book I grabbed was *Men Explain Things to Me* by Rebecca Solnit, which I'd already read once. I put it in my bag and headed to a meeting. On the subway, I opened the book, and immediately became aware of the gaze of the men around me. I felt like their eyes were burning holes through the cover, which is a basic blue square with no image, just the title printed in large, white letters, like a billboard, MEN EXPLAIN THINGS TO ME. I kept my head down, and quietly read my book, trying to ignore the tension the imposing title seemed to be creating. Then, after only a minute of silent reading, a man's finger planted itself in the middle of the page of my book. He was pointing to the words, "Women Strike for Peace."

I was startled and snapped my head up, to find a very tall man leaning over me, into me, his head positioned next to mine, so he could also read the book I was reading. This was such a strangely invasive move on an uncrowded train that others around me also snapped to attention, shooting the man "what the fuck?" looks. This in no way dissuaded him.

"I just wanna say something," he told me. "You see this? You shouldn't have to do that." He spoke with a Jamaican accent. He was well-dressed in a white polo shirt and dress pants, his hair in locks, and a Jamaican flag necklace adorning his neck. He smiled at me sweetly, and ran his finger across the lines again, totally up in my space, just touching my book.

"Women shouldn't have to strike for peace. You shouldn't have to withhold . . . *that*" (he placed his hand to his chest, tenderly) "from us to get us to stop fighting."

I stared at him, perplexed for a moment, then realized what was happening, and what he meant. He thought this line was about a female sex strike. I didn't know where to begin. Should I demand he lean back, get his hand off my book, get out of my personal space? Probably, but instead, I corrected him, and said, "No. It's not about . . . *sex.* 'Women Strike for Peace' is the name of an antinuclear women's activist group from the sixties."

"Yeah," he said, again, "But you shouldn't have to do that. Women shouldn't have to withhold that for us to be peaceful. We should give it" [peace] "to you because you are our mothers."

Was this really fucking happening? The book I was reading is *about* men incorrectly explaining things they know nothing of to women who actually know something about the subject they are being incorrectly lectured on. I was reading this to get some ideas for the introduction to the book I was writing about times men invaded my space in a sexist manner, and here I was, just sitting on the subway, quietly reading to myself, when this stranger started up. How ironic can you get?

"No." I said again. "'Women Strike for Peace' is the name of an anti-war group from the sixties. They were against nuclear arms. It's not about sex. It's about nuclear war, and *strike* means, like, protest."

"Oh, I thought this was about men and women," he said, taking my book while it was still in my hand, and flipping it, and pointing to the title on the cover.

At this point, the people sitting across from me on the subway were watching us, wide-eyed, engrossed. "I just want to elevate women," he said, "because I come from you."

"Well, no," I mumbled. "I'm not your mom." I laughed nervously.

"We *all* come from you!" he insisted. "Women are goddesses. You know what I mean? I want to raise women up, because we all come from women."

"Sure," I nodded, "And men. We all come from men, too."

"No," he said, gesturing to my stomach/womb area, "We all come from *you*. You are *mother*."

"I'm not a mother," I said dryly.

"But you have potential," he said.

"Okay, well, I guess . . . hmmm . . . you mean that as a nice sentiment," I said, wanting to end the conversation.

He stared at me expectantly. "I *love* women. We all come from you. Women are *mother*. You are mother."

"Umm. Thanks. See ya," I tried.

The train stopped and the door opened, and he headed for the door, and then he turned to me and said, "I love women. You *are* mother. Okay. Understand?" Then he smiled and blew me a kiss, and told me, "You're welcome."

As soon as the door closed behind him, two women near me started squealing with laughter and shaking their heads. One woman pointed to my book and clapped her hands and laughed and said, "They just can't! They *just can't*!"

"No, they can't," I agreed, also laughing so hard my eyes were tearing up.

That's all we said, but we all knew what we meant. *They just can't* . . . resist . . . explaining things to us!

I posted this story on social media, and it went viral. Some people responded negatively, saying I misunderstood him, and he was trying to be anti-sexist. "He was trying to be nice. He was trying to connect."

Both of these things are true. This was not a traumatic event, and he thought he was being nice, maybe even generous.

But, to spell it out, touching someone's book over their shoulder multiple times, without so much as speaking to them, is invasive. I doubt he would have done it to a man.

He perceived an intimacy with me, and felt he should be able to access my space, because I am a woman.

He had no idea what the line he was pointing to was about. I actually had to repeat this three or four times, before he (not listened to me, but) relented and moved on to his "compliments," because he didn't care what the book was about. He invaded my space and pawed my book like it was his, because he wanted an "in" with me. He took the title of the book as an indictment of men, and he wanted me to recognize him as a good man. He wanted to win me over. This man I'd never seen before and probably will never see again wanted me to give him my affection and attention.

If he'd struck up an actual conversation, told me that was an interesting title, and *asked me* what the book was about, that could maybe have been a nice interaction. But that's not what he did, and he didn't really want to know.

This wasn't about me, or the book. It was about him. He wanted to be seen as a good man, who loves women . . . as mothers. I am not a mother. I probably will never be a mother. I don't want to be seen as a mother, especially not a mother to every man. I don't like that. It's not a compliment. It's belittling and reductive.

I don't want men to "lift women up" because we are prosaic mother figures, or sisters, daughters, or wives. I don't want men to lift me up at all. I want to stand on equal ground, because I am a human deserving total equality, regardless of my sex or gender. I want men to respect my boundaries and my intellect, as much as they do other men's . . . to be clear.

I have cataloged one hundred instances of these types of experiences. I have seen that men of all races, classes, creeds, and nationalities are equally guilty of this type of behavior.

In this book, I've written clear descriptions of my experiences of sexism, because these things that happen repeatedly to women are systematically allowed, encouraged, and built into our social norms, globally. These experiences shape us as people from the time we are born (or come out/transition to living) as female, and they happen *because* we are female. I am talking about what has happened to me because I am a woman. Over and over again. All of my life.

I've written about times I was touched sexually without my consent, assaulted violently, threatened, had my body invaded, or was demeaned or controlled, and I knew it was specifically because I am a woman. And I'm not talking about flirtation or "making a move." I am not even talking about explicit "come-ons" or overtly sexual propositions in normal hookup-inclined social spaces like bars and clubs and parties, or all the things people do, sometimes awkwardly, to try to get it on, which I am fond of myself, and which is a wonderful aspect of being human. And I am not talking about consensual sex at all, good or bad. And to be clear, most women, when we share our experiences of sexism, are not talking about those things.

It has been an upward battle to even find the way to say what I've needed to say for so long. But, I've found clarity through simplicity. I am, after all, a storyteller. Though the bulk of my writing and publications have been relegated to the realm of fiction, when I speak to people I'm close to, in order to illustrate a point, I immediately go to stories from my own life. That is my natural inclination, and that is where my strengths lie. When I am not sure how to explain why or how something came to be, I can always, at least, describe what happened clearly, honestly, and precisely.

Through social media movements like #MeToo and YesAllWomen, women have spoken together to raise awareness of *how many* of us have experienced sexual harassment, violence, and assault. But what the movements have not made apparent is *how often* women have these experiences. Beyond this, sexual harassment and assault are only symptoms of a much deeper problem. The impact of sexism on the everyday lives of women goes beyond *sexual violence*, and so should the conversation. This is why I've also included instances of blatant discrimination, times when I walked away knowing that I was being treated a certain way simply *because* I was a woman.

I am sharing this dark list, these stories, because the majority of women I know have such a list, if they start to think about it. And that is entirely my point. It's not that *my* life has been *exceptionally* plagued with sexism. It's that it hasn't. That is exactly why I wrote this.

It's my hope that men will read this book and come away with a greater understanding of how sexism shapes women, of the cumulative impact it has, that may otherwise remain invisible to many men.

And as upsetting as some of the stories in this book may be to read, all of these things actually happened to me. One woman. One person. And remember, I still haven't written about *every* time sexism carved something out of me, permanently reshaping me. I've only written one hundred times.

1

When I was five years old, I was playing in the sprinklers in my swimming suit with a five-year-old boy. He kept pinching my butt to the point that I started crying. I repeatedly told him to stop, and finally retaliated by hitting him. He didn't stop. He kept doing it, chasing me and pinching my butt harder and harder, until it actually hurt. When I went inside and told on him, his mother laughed at me and told me I probably liked it. Almost all of the adults present thought it was cute.

I learned quickly that if a boy was hurting me, he would get in trouble. But, if the way he was hurting me was sexual, I would be mocked, and it would be assumed I'd secretly enjoyed this assault.

2

When I was five years old, I was digging in the dirt with another boy in his front yard. He had a knife and small shovel and I was just using my hands to dig. I asked if I could use one of his digging tools, the knife or the shovel. He said I couldn't have either because girls shouldn't dig. His mother made him give me one.

He gave me the small shovel, and we both kept digging, but he was glaring at me, and then he reached over and stabbed my hand with his knife. It was the worst physical pain I'd felt so far in my young life. He cut me deeply, and my hand was bleeding. He said it was an accident. It wasn't an accident.

3

A boy got into a physical altercation with me when I was six years old, over a ThunderCats sword. I lived with my paternal grandparents primarily, from the age of two. I was shopping with my grandmother, and she told me I could pick out one toy that day. I picked a plastic ThunderCats sword (the last one) and I was carrying it around when a boy came up to me, shoved me, and tried to wrestle the sword away from me. He told me swords weren't for girls, and that ThunderCats hated girls.

He said that *he* was going to have his mom buy the sword for him. When he was unable to wrestle the sword away from me, he was still so certain that I wasn't going to be able to actually buy the sword that he followed me to my grandmother and told her that swords weren't for girls. She informed him that this was my sword because I had it first, and she said that I could pick one toy that day. Then she took the sword and told me to put it in her cart, and we left.

4

In the second grade, I raised my hand in PE. I was wearing a tank top. The male gym teacher said, "Oh yeah, I can see it, baby, hubba hubba," in a goofy sexy voice, and leaned down and motioned to my chest. I looked down and realized he was referring to my nipple, which I noticed was poking slightly out of my tank top. I was six years old and had no breasts. I'd never felt embarrassed about my nipples showing before, or thought of my chest as sexual. I was deeply embarrassed in that moment, because of the way my adult male teacher decided to talk to me in front of all of my classmates.

I don't think this man is evil or anything. I don't think he's a pedophile. He just didn't think twice about jokingly sexualizing a young girl, because this is so normalized. The impact on me, though, was to make me overly aware and ashamed of my body, especially of my chest, which I had never even previously been aware of as a possibly sexual part of my six-year-old body. He also seemed to be jokingly implying I was "showing him" my nipple on purpose.

5

When I was seven, I was playing with a group of neighborhood boys outside, while staying for a week with my mother's family. We were in a trailer park playing in the parking lot. I was the only girl. At first, we were all having fun, pretending to hide and find imaginary treasure, and rolling and jumping off things. The game suddenly and inexplicably turned into all of the boys attacking me.

They decided the game should be to capture and torture me. They hit me with sticks, they shoved me, they chased me. This went beyond play, very quickly. They were really hurting me. In a panic, I found an unlocked car in the parking lot, crawled inside, and locked myself in. I was terrified. I was screaming and crying. They were laughing and banging on the doors. I stayed locked in the car long enough that they finally got bored and went away.

When they were gone, I got out of the car, went inside, and told the adults what had happened. The adults (my aunts and uncles) laughed at me and told me that I probably liked the attention from all of the boys. I wanted to go outside and play again, but I was too afraid to leave the house that day. I also knew if the boys did come back while I was outside, I wouldn't be able to get an adult to help, because it had already been implied that this was something I probably enjoyed, and therefore, had encouraged. In other words, this was my fault.

6

In the third grade, five or six boys ran by me on the playground and snapped my bra strap. They all swarmed me and snapped my bra strap, one after the other, because it was the first day that I'd ever worn a bra. They did this to *every* girl the first day they noticed her wearing a bra. It didn't bother me so much, honestly. I was expecting it. I'd known it was eventually going to happen to me for about a year, and accepted it, strangely, as a rite of passage. But some of my girlfriends were so upset they cried when they found out they had to start wearing a bra, because they feared and hated this ritual.

One of my best friends was especially upset about it. She was eleven years old when she developed breasts, and when she was finally given a bra by her mother, she had a small breakdown. I remember sitting in her bedroom, her holding my hand, tears running down her cheeks, saying, "Please don't let them do that to me, Chavisa. I can't stand it if they do that to me." I was surprised by this reaction, because my best friend in grade school and I were an odd couple. I was dorky, religious, bookish, and strange. She was a popular, beautiful blond athlete, a star of the basketball team, and much more physically fit and capable than I was. I thought, if she was mad at the boys, she could physically fight them, or outrun them, or tell them off and they would actually care. But she was asking *me* for protection.

The next day, she showed up to school wearing a bra, which we could all tell, because it was summer and you could easily see the outline of the straps through her shirt. I told other girls how upset she was, and her close friends, as well as girls who didn't know her well, became angry. They all got the same determined look on their faces and said, "Don't worry. We won't let them bother her." That day on the playground, many, many girls and one of her more effeminate close male friends stood around her keeping her between us the entire recess. We noticed some of the boys gathering, pointing, and talking, sometimes, no doubt, about "getting her," but they didn't, because they couldn't have gotten through us if they'd tried.

7

I was ten years old and selling candies, cookies, and cheeses door-to-door to raise money for the school band, as all the band kids did every year. Mine was a close-knit, quiet rural neighborhood. I knocked on a neighbor's door. The man of the family, who I knew casually, answered the door. His wife and kids were gone. He ordered some candy and gave me a large bill. I didn't have change on me, so I went across the street to my house to get some dollar bills.

When I returned, he opened the door, and he was wearing nothing but blue men's bikini bottoms, which he had pulled down in the front so that his penis was fully exposed, and was right in my face because of our height difference and where I was standing on his stoop.

He began asking me casual questions about his candy order. I held his money up to him, stunned. He didn't take it for a while, but kept talking, with his exposed penis in my face. I felt terrified, frozen. I was confused about the nature of what was happening, because I was ten years old, and he was in his forties, and he was acting like he wasn't doing anything out of the ordinary. I'd been warned about men being inappropriate with me, but I'd always pictured them as grotesque strangers, creepily attempting to lure me in or initiating some physical struggle to abduct or rape me. I'd never imagined a man I'd known for years would just casually place his penis in my face while chatting about the weather.

I stood silently, holding the money up to him as he talked. He finally took the money from my hand and tried to keep talking to me, but as soon as he took the bills, I turned and ran away.

8

When I was eleven years old, I lost one of my
closest friends because I was a girl and he was a boy. My
next-door neighbor, let's call him Mike, and I had been
friends since we were toddlers. There weren't any other kids
in our neighborhood, and even though we were almost two
years apart in age (he was older), we were very close. I grew
up in the country, outside the limits of our small town. Our
yards were connected and extended into miles of cornfields
and woods. We liked to play baseball together, and shoot BB
guns and bows and arrows. Often, we would bury things—
soldiers, Barbies, coins, toy cars, play jewelry—and draw
maps to mark the location of things we'd buried, like pirate
treasure maps, then wait several weeks and try to forget
where we'd buried what, and use the maps to find them, and
dig them up again. This was one of my favorite pastimes.

When I was in the first grade, another boy was sometimes
in the neighborhood because his mom was providing home
care for an elderly neighbor. He began playing with us, but
he was mostly obsessed with me. He was always pinching
my butt, pinching my side, trying to get me to kiss him, and
asking me to be his girlfriend. He didn't want to play the
way Mike and I had always played. He wanted me to show
him "mine" and he wanted to show me "his." This is all fine

and dandy kids' stuff, but I didn't want to, and his behavior around me also made Mike very uncomfortable.

One day, Mike, the new boy, and I were burying something together by my swing set, and Mike and I were talking about what coordinates we should put on the map to find the treasure, and the new boy interrupted us. He grabbed my hand and kissed it and told me he loved me. He asked me to kiss him on the lips, and said if I kissed him on the lips, that would make me his girlfriend. I said something like, "Aw, come on. Would you stop it? I don't want to," and huffed, embarrassed.

And then Mike surprised me. He jammed his toy shovel in the dirt and said to the boy, "This is so annoying. We just want to play. We've been playing for years, and we always had a good time. We have a good thing here, and then you come around with all this romance crap and . . ." He took a deep breath, then he yelled, "You're ruining *everything*!"

We told the kid that if he didn't cut it out, he couldn't play with us anymore. And he actually left, finally, I think because a boy had told him this time.

That made me feel closer to Mike. He had my back. He saw me as an equal. He valued my friendship. And of course, it meant something to me that an older boy respected me and valued my friendship as much as I did his. We kept playing that way for years.

Then, when I was eleven, and he was thirteen, things began to shift. If I had friends over, he wouldn't come play with us anymore, unless it was to scare or tease us. One day, one of his male friends was over, who was a boy just a year older than me. I knew him pretty well, because we attended a small school. I was bored, and walked over to Mike's house to hang out, and this boy greeted me on the porch as I was walking up. He stood pointing a gun at me. "Take one more step and I'll shoot," he told me. "No girls allowed."

He walked down off the porch, and met me at the border

of my yard and Mike's yard. His gun was a high-powered pellet gun that looked like a machine gun. It couldn't kill anything but small animals, but it could put an eye out. He pointed it at my head. "What are you doing? I'm just here to see Mike," I told him.

"We're playing, and there are no girls allowed," he warned me again. "Take one more step and I'll shoot."

I rolled my eyes, and took one step forward, defiantly, and he shot me. It was at very close range, though he only shot me in the foot, but the pellet went through my shoe and broke the skin. I crumpled to the ground, grabbed my foot, and started wailing. The boy who had shot me, suddenly went from brave assassin to scared little boy. "No, no no no," he told me, "I'm sorry, I'm sorry, I'm sorry." He got down on the ground and tried to put his hand over my mouth, but that just made me squeal louder and pull away. I was, after all, an eleven-year-old girl, and the pellet really stung, but what stung even worse was that he'd had the gall to shoot me, just for coming over to say hi. I think the crying was about 20 percent from actual pain, and the rest was hurt feelings and bruised ego.

Hearing my screams, Mike and his parents ran out of the house. Of course, it was obvious immediately what had happened. The gun was lying on the ground. There was a pellet-sized hole in my shoe. I also told them repeatedly, "He shot me. He *shot* me!"

Mike came over for a visit a few days later. He was more serious than I'd ever seen him and said he wanted to talk to me. We went into my yard and sat on the large lawn swing. He told me that his friend had gotten in big trouble because I told on him. He told me the kid's dad had hit him, and worse. He'd picked him up and slammed him, shirtless, down on a metal picnic table (in the middle of a hot summer day) while he beat him. His friend had burn marks on his back in the pattern of the metal table. "That's what he got for shooting a sweet little girl," Mike told me. "It was some show you put on," he told me. "It couldn't have hurt that bad."

I argued with him. I told him I just wanted to visit, like always, and he'd shot me for no good reason. I told him, "It *did* hurt." The truth was, it did hurt, but I cried more than it physically hurt. My crying wasn't an affectation, though. It came naturally to a kid with a bleeding foot and hurt feelings. I didn't make myself cry more on purpose.

He wasn't having it. He was mad at me for crying about getting shot. He told me that what his friend's dad had done was my fault.

I balked at this. "His dad's crazy. That's awful. But he's the one who shot me. It's not my fault his dad beat him up," I said, firmly, and then, Mike smacked me in the face, hard. With his right hand, he smacked me hard on my left cheek. It turned my head to the side. My hair hung in my face. I stared coldly down at the ground. He sat looking at me sternly. I didn't cry. I didn't scream. I didn't say anything else, and neither did he. I just brushed my hair out of my face, and stood silently without looking back, and walked into my house. I felt like a woman then. We were growing up. Our friendship would never be the same. I was becoming a woman, and at thirteen, he was becoming a man.

9

When I was eleven, my grandmother on my mother's side died of a heart attack. This was a preventable death. When she began experiencing chest pains, she knew she was having a heart attack, and she immediately had her son drive her to the emergency room. She was fifty years old. She told the doctor that she thought she was having a heart attack. The male doctor told her that it was probably pains related to menopause, and that she was only having muscle spasms. He prescribed her Tylenol and sent her home. She died at her house, lying on the couch, holding her chest, about an hour after she was released from the emergency room.

My family sued. Another family, who'd also lost a female family member because of the same mistake made by the same doctor, also sued. Both families were suing to have the doctor's license taken away. Though my family won the suit against the doctor, and my mother and her siblings received a small amount of money from the suit, the doctor kept his license. And of course, my mom and her siblings lost a mother, and I lost a grandmother, and my grandmother lost her life very young.

Through the yearlong suit, I learned that doctors misdiagnosing heart problems as "female troubles" in women is quite common. In this case, sexism is actually deadly.

In the seventh grade, when I had begun noticeably developing larger breasts, a boy who was walking past me through the empty high school gymnasium stepped in front of me, blocking my path, and punched me, with both of his fists landing on my chest.

He directly punched both of my breasts as hard as he could, straight on, and left me lying on the floor, gasping in pain.

When I was able to gather myself, I immediately went to a teacher, and she laughed at me. She asked if I liked the attention. I had tears in my eyes, and I was holding my chest. I guess she thought I was being melodramatic, but I was persistent. She finally took me more seriously and told me the next time it happened that I should kick him in the balls. I insisted that I needed to go to the nurse or the principal. I told the nurse and the principal what had happened. The female nurse was actually deeply concerned, but the male principal didn't understand *why* the boy had done this or the magnitude of the assault. There were no witnesses, and the boy was never punished for what he did.

11

When I was twelve years old, a friend of my mother's, a fifty-year-old man, began talking to me while I was standing away from the crowd at a family barbecue held by my mother's side of the family. This older man told me I was beautiful and that I had my mother's hips, and asked me if I wanted to go on a boat ride with him. I said I would love to, and that I didn't even know he owned a boat.

He said he had a big boat and that the motor purrs, then he pursed his lips and "blew raspberries," making a fake motor sound with his lips. I was confused. He laughed and asked again if I wanted a boat ride from him. I didn't answer. He explained to me that a "boat ride" is when a man puts his lips "down there" on a girl (he pointed to my crotch), and "blows raspberries," and it feels good.

12

In the seventh grade, between classes at our lockers, the same boy who had punched me in the breasts repeatedly told me to suck his dick and grabbed the back of my head and shoved me toward his crotch. Later that day, also in the busy hallway, he loudly called me a whore. That humiliated me even more than him grabbing me and pushing me toward his crotch. I cried in front of everyone.

Several girls took me to the bathroom, washed my face, and tried to talk me into physically attacking him. I refused, because I didn't believe in physical violence at the time. I considered myself a pacifist. The girls did the best they could to comfort me. Even girls who I somewhat considered childhood enemies were nice to me that day.

13

In the eighth grade, the same boy who'd punched me in the chest was in history class with me. He got up to sharpen his pencil. The pencil sharpener was near my desk. He held his large history book under his arm, and, as he was walking past me, he took the history book and swung it hard, hitting me in the back of the head. My head went down, and my face slammed into my desk. I blacked out for a second, and when I came to, he was sharpening his pencil casually, as if nothing had happened. All the kids were chattering and turned toward me. Blood was coming out of my nose. I started crying.

The teacher had turned away from the board and was staring at me, a look of total befuddlement on his face. He asked what had happened. The boy was standing near me, glaring at me, as if daring me to tell on him. Through my gasps and tears, I told the teacher the boy had hit me with his large history book, which he was still holding. My classmates murmured agreements, seeming stunned by the whole incident. The teacher still looked confused. "I didn't see it," he said. "I didn't see anything. I can't do anything."

He sent me to the nurse. The boy, again, didn't get in trouble. I even went to my teacher the next day, to recount what he'd done, and my male teacher told me the boy probably had a crush on me.

Years later, when I was nineteen, I ran into the boy in a gas station, and he told me that I looked like a freak now (I was Goth), and that he'd always had a crush on me. I told him I thought he was a prick and that I always hated him and still did. He tormented me (and a few other girls) constantly for two years throughout junior high, until he moved away. I've only written here the most violent things he did to me.

It doesn't matter if he had a crush on me. *Why* he did this doesn't matter. What mattered is the impact it had on me.

What sort of lesson is it to teach girls that being physically assaulted by a boy is a sign of love?

Dozens of times, from the eighth grade on, teachers and administrators stopped me in the hallway to check and see how short my skirt was, or to make me put on a jacket or a different shirt because my shoulders were not fully covered, or because I had "too much" cleavage showing, because I was wearing a tank top in the summertime and had large breasts. Boys though, regularly wore jerseys in the summertime, with nothing under them. Sometimes they wore such baggy jerseys that we could actually see their nipples, and that was fine. But I wasn't allowed to wear a tank top.

Being stopped regularly and having my clothing checked was beyond insulting and drove home the idea that I may have in some way provoked anything that happened to me. It was also a total joke, because my clothing never mattered. When I was assaulted or sexually harassed in school, I was almost always wearing regulation clothing, sometimes full-length jeans and sweatshirts. It was pretty fucked up to experience and witness girls being so regularly sexually harassed and assaulted by boys, and then, on top of this, being publicly shamed by the school staff for being female, having bodies, and wearing typical summer clothing. It drove home our place in the pecking order on a level that I think had a deep subconscious impact on all of the students, male and female.

When I was thirteen years old, I played an informal football game in my friend's front yard every weekend for a couple of months. It was a mixed-gender game and the boys *tagged* the girls, but *tackled* each other.

Most of the boys were my friends or schoolmates. I told them I wanted to play regular football and that they could tackle me like they did all the other boys, and they could expect me to do the same, because it was boring just getting tagged and having to stop running and give over the ball. I felt that it was unfair that I had to stop running because a boy lightly tagged me. I should have a chance to try to keep going with the football and gain more yards, and make them really stop me, so I could sometimes get farther. That is, after all, the whole point of the game. All the guys agreed to tackle me like they did each other, without argument, except for one. One of the boys had a major problem with this.

He argued with me, and I argued back. I was stubborn and said I wanted to be treated like one of the guys.

The next time the football was thrown to me, as I was running with the ball, this boy ran up behind me and punched me in the lower back. I stopped and gasped, and then he shoved me with both of his hands and I fell on my face, and he jumped on top of me, lying on my back, and grabbed hold of me and slammed me into the ground repeatedly. He then pressed all of his weight against me, lying on my back, and whispered in my ear, "You sure want to be treated like one of the guys?"

Of course, I'd never seen one of the guys get kidney-punched in the back by another guy while playing football. I'd never seen them get jumped on that way after they were already down. I never saw another guy pounce on them after they were down, and start slamming them into the ground, then lie on top of them while they were still gasping from pain and whisper shitty things in their ear.

That's the moment I learned that if I wanted to be treated like one of the guys, I was going to be treated much, much harsher than the guys.

I understood why. This boy didn't want me to think I was capable of doing what he did. It was wildly threatening to him to give me a chance, because that would mean a girl could do the same thing as him, and, I suppose, that would mean he was no better than a girl. I never played football with them again.

16

When I was fourteen years old, I was walking in the mall, holding hands with my grandma, and a group of boys walked up to us and started yelling loudly that they wanted to fuck me in the ass, repeatedly. Then they laughed and laughed and laughed.

17

When I was fourteen years old, a man in his thirties who was in an authority position working with children and teenagers at the local community theater, where I acted in many plays, attacked me, held me down, and tried to rape me.

This was an intense physical altercation. I barely knew him, and this happened within the first five minutes the first time I was ever in a room alone with him.

He was the theater and lighting technician and was supposed to be giving me a private lesson on running the lighting board.

Many other students had signed up for and received lessons from him after rehearsals. He and I were alone in a small tech booth together, and there was only one other person in the entire building, which was quite large.

I weighed about one hundred pounds when I was fourteen, and he was an adult male in his early thirties. I remember, this day I was wearing a skirt and nylon pantyhose. I was sitting on my knees next to him (he was also on his knees, because the booth was so small) at the light board. I'd been with him for only a few minutes. All I'd really said was "hello." As he began explaining how to work the lights, he grabbed my ankle and then pulled me toward him, knocked me on my back, and got on top of me. He held me down with his arm across my chest. Then he started running his hand up my leg, until he got it under my skirt, and then he started touching me sexually.

At first, I froze, but my mother is also a sexual assault survivor, and had told me from a young age that this might happen to me someday. She always told me, whatever I did, to try not to freeze. I didn't even know what she meant when she told me that. But the first thing I did when this happened was freeze. It was hard to unfreeze. I was completely confused and terrified, and everything in my body had suddenly "frozen," something I'd never experienced so clearly before.

This man was an adult, an authority figure. And something I can never get out of my head, that I think also caused me to freeze, was that the whole time he was knocking me over, holding me down, and touching me, he kept calmly talking about the lights. He kept explaining to me how to work the lighting board, as if he were still giving me a lesson in theater tech. It was surreal. (Years after, I've realized that he probably did this in case the one other person in the building came near the small room we were in. He would hear the man teaching me the ins and outs of theater tech and assume everything was fine.)

I couldn't find my voice, but I finally began kicking my legs and scooting backward. It was such a weird feeling; I felt physically unable to speak or yell. I wiggled and scooted back, wrestling with him. He kept holding me down, pulled at me, and tugged at my tights trying to get them off. But I kept kicking and scooting back and was somehow able to get him off me, or, at least, get myself mostly out from under him. I turned and crawled out of the booth, stood, and ran to the wooden ladder that led down from the lighting booth into the theater office.

He was up, and coming after me, and he yelled, in a deep, commanding voice, "Stop. Wait." And I did.

And even writing this, I cannot believe I did, but maybe

I can believe it, because I was a girl who hated getting in trouble, and when an adult gave me orders, I instinctively did what they said. I was also terrified of him. I was barely fourteen. I was more of a child than I realized then. I stopped, I waited, panting, bent over, my hand reaching for the first rung of the ladder, keeping my eyes on him. He walked casually up to me and said, simply, "I'll go down first. I'll hold the ladder in case you fall."

I stepped back. He descended the ladder, then stood at the bottom, holding it, which was pointless because it was connected at the top and folded up into the lighting booth, so it couldn't actually fall. I came down the ladder after him. Like I said, I was wearing a short skirt and sheer pantyhose. As I descended the ladder, I could feel him looking up my skirt, and he began saying things to me about my panties. "I can see it. I like your sexy panties. I like that," and so on. As soon as I got down the ladder, I pushed past him, bolted out the office door, grabbed my things from the chair in the lobby, and ran to the parking lot, where my grandmother was already waiting, early to pick me up.

When I saw her car, I was, at that moment, certain I was going to run to her and tell her everything that had just happened. But when I got to the car, I saw my boyfriend at the time sitting in the front passenger seat with my grandma, and I sank suddenly, down into some silent hole inside of myself that I never knew existed.

There were several reasons for this. I didn't want my boyfriend to know what this man had done. I would have been deeply ashamed for him to know that, and, also, I thought he might go in and kill the guy, or beat him up badly, and go to jail (my boyfriend was two years older, sixteen, and was well-built enough to have possibly hurt this man badly).

Also, my grandmother had recently discovered that I wasn't a virgin. I'd been sexually active with my boyfriend, and she was upset about this. (To be clear, I had a good relationship with my boyfriend and was a very willing participant in our sexual activity.) But because she'd found out I wasn't a virgin, there had been several months of intense division between my grandmother, my boyfriend, and me. My grandmother is very religious, and I also became sexually active unusually young. The fact that my boyfriend was in the car, and they were both smiling, was a sign that things were maybe being mended. I got in the back of the car and they both turned and smiled at me. My boyfriend was beaming. He winked at me. Yes, he was trying to mend things with my grandma, obviously, which he knew was important to me. A wave of intense guilt came over me. I was young, and I wasn't a virgin, and my grandma hated that, and I was wearing a skirt that my grandma thought was too short, and it all suddenly felt to me like I'd definitely been asking for this man to rape me. So I didn't say anything to anyone.

Months after the attack, rumors began to stir that the lighting technician who assaulted me was having an affair with a fifteen-year-old student, who he had appointed as his tech assistant. I saw her in the lighting booth with him often, and I did see them, when they thought no one was looking, holding hands and exchanging brief kisses. It was clear that the rumors were most likely true and that he was sleeping with her, but I thought of this as different than what he'd done to me. Though it was technically illegal, I thought of it as consensual, because she seemed to like it.

Still, the lighting tech assaulted at least two other girls while working in the local theater and drama club. The girls were ages thirteen and fifteen at the time of the assaults. Over the year after he assaulted me, these girls ended up telling me their stories.

We came together because whenever he was around, the three of us all got noticeably as far away from him as possible. He also worked as a theater tech at the neighboring high school where I attended drama club, and where these girls were students. (My small, rural school didn't have a drama club, so I attended drama club at this larger school one town over from mine.) It wasn't hard for us to put two and two together, when, every time he came into the school theater, we all went and sat as far away from the stage as possible, in the chairs in the back of the theater, and watched him.

It's amazing to me how vividly I can remember pieces of this, like a movie reel that plays in my head. I was sitting in the back on the far right of the theater, and the other girls were near me, and he was on the stage, hammering a piece of wood with the other students milling around the stage. The two other girls and I were sitting far away from him, near each other, all glaring at him. I said, "I hate him." And one of the other girls said, "I hate him, too." And the other girl said, "Me too. Why do you hate him?"

We shared our stories over and over for days. The older girl in the group, who was sixteen at the time we began talking about our assaults, became insistent that we should turn him in when she found out how far he'd gone with me. With the two of them, his assaults had not gone further than lifting one girl's skirt and smacking her ass, grabbing the other girl's breasts, and repeated sexual comments. Eventually, I agreed to report him to a teacher, if the other girls would do it with me. I didn't want to be the only one telling my story. We did this privately, through a female teacher.

We approached our teacher after drama club rehearsal, when we could be alone with her. We told her that this man had tried to rape me and had also touched the other two girls sexually. The teacher said to us, "These are serious allegations. Are you sure all of this is true? Are you sure you want to do this?" I was shocked by this response, because I was close to this teacher. I looked up to her. I thought we had a good relationship, and she seemed angry, but not necessarily with the man who assaulted us, and suddenly, for the first time ever, skeptical of my integrity. She said sternly, almost coldly, "Okay. I'll take this seriously. It'll be dealt with."

I had no idea what to expect. I didn't see the man who'd assaulted me in the community theater or drama club again. A few weeks passed. I assumed it had been taken care of. Then, one day, I was pulled out of PE by my guidance counselor and taken to a small room, where my male high school principal, Mr. Smith, was waiting with another man I'd never seen before and never saw again. They closed the door and asked me to sit in a chair against the wall, facing them. The three adults stared at me, and my female guidance counselor told me that they knew I was accusing a man of attempted rape. The man I'd never seen before was helping conduct an internal investigation. I do not remember if he was a lawyer or social worker, but I believe he was with the Illinois Department of Child and Family Services (DCFS). I do not believe this was clearly explained to me at the time, if at all, and, if it was, I did not understand it.

This man sat in a chair and scooted close to me. He told me he'd already interviewed the two other girls, and that he needed to get some details from me about what I'd experienced.

I was devastated. I hadn't told my high school guidance counselor or principal. I had only told a teacher from a school in a nearby town, where I attended drama club. I hadn't wanted people in my small hometown to know. I was completely unaware that my turning this man in could result in my own school staff knowing what had happened. I thought, for a moment, of telling them that nothing that bad had happened, and to forget it, that I had exaggerated, or that the teacher from the other school had misunderstood.

I was sweaty, still in my gym clothes—short, red cotton shorts and a white shirt—and I felt exposed. I wondered if I looked bad. I wanted to go and change back into my regular clothes and fix my hair and makeup. I wondered if they would believe this man tried to rape me if I didn't look good. I asked them if I could go change back into my regular clothes first. They told me, "That isn't necessary." My principal told me I didn't "need" to change into regular clothes before I described the attempted rape I experienced. It would have made me feel more comfortable, calm, and in control, but I'm sure that didn't occur to them. I was fourteen years old, and they were my authority figures. I didn't think of myself as a victim of a crime who had any rights, or whose comfort in this situation mattered. I was a kid obeying directions from my principal and teachers.

The man I didn't know asked me about the dates and location of the attack. Then he told me to tell him exactly what happened in my own words; to recount every detail I could remember. I felt like I was going to throw up. Asking me to do this in front of my principal felt like they might as well have been asking me to stand up and take off my pants and show them my cunt.

But I *did* tell them, and it was awful to have to say to these adults that a man held me down and put his hand up my skirt and touched me, "where exactly?" the man I didn't know asked.

"My vagina." I told him, struggling to hold my head up and look him in the eye.

"Over your underwear, or under?"

"He touched my vagina, over my underwear." These words were horrible to have to say. I felt dizzy and dry mouthed, like I was confessing to something insanely nasty I'd done.

When I finished, the man I didn't know asked me to tell him what the other girls had claimed happened to them. I told him. He sighed and looked to the floor. "That's exactly what they said," he told the principal and guidance counselor.

So, that was what an internal investigation consists of, and that was enough evidence to take the case to court, if I wanted.

The man I didn't know told me he was sorry that had

happened to me and that I was being "very mature about all this. You're a very mature young woman." And I'm sure he was actually moved by what I'd said. He was compassionate with me. But for some reason, I always remember him saying that specifically, "You're being very mature about all this. You're a very mature young woman," and I think he meant it as comfort or as a compliment, but there's something that feels strange to me about that, my being "mature about it." I didn't know what he meant at the time, and I still don't.

They told me that no matter what I decided, the man who attacked me would be fired and would never be allowed to work with children again.

I was asked once if I wanted to contact the police, press charges, and take him to court, and I said I didn't want anyone to know about this, and the adults involved seemed happy and relieved about that. I thought, if this became public, most people would think this was my fault, something I had actually wanted, or that I was lying for attention.

The man who tried to rape me was quietly fired from working in the schools and community theater.

Three years later, he was hired back to the same community theater to do lighting tech for a play in which I was the female lead. I ran into him in the hallway. I was so upset, I left abruptly, drove my car into a ditch, and vomited. The next day, I told an adult who I was close to at the community theater, a gay male, what had happened a few years before. He took it seriously, and this man was immediately fired, again.

18

Months after I reported this man for attacking me and
holding me down and attempting to rape me, I was taking
part in community theater activities with a group of students.
The first teacher/director I had reported the assault to, one of
the few people who knew this had happened to me, asked for
some volunteers to go to the prop room and carry some tables
and chairs down. A boy who was my friend raised his hand,
and I raised mine. The teacher asked for another male volunteer, instead. I balked. "I'm strong enough to carry tables," I
told her. She then told another boy to go up, took me aside,
and said, "Think about this. Do you really want to go into a
room alone with that boy? You don't want to get yourself in
trouble again, do you?"

I felt like dying and smacking her all at the same time when
she said that, and I've never forgotten it. I have nothing but
the utmost love and admiration for this woman, still. I don't
think she's a bad person, at all. I understand this is a common,
wrongheaded mentality. But even in that moment at that age, I
knew better. It made me angry. I thought, "I didn't *get myself* in
trouble." I signed up to take a tutoring session to learn theater
tech, which many other kids did, and the man who was supposed
to be teaching me, as soon as I sat next to him, grabbed my ankle,
knocked me over, held me down, and tried to *rape* me.

I've spent hundreds of hours alone with men. All of my male grade school, junior high, and high school teachers, sports coaches, music instructors, theater directors, pianist accompanists, male friends and acquaintances; in all sorts of circumstances, had reason to find themselves alone in a room with me at some point. I had no trouble with them, *because they didn't try to rape me!*

It was a total mind-fuck that people would be afraid to be *alone* with *me*, and with *women*, because of what some *men did* to *us*.

*   *   *

I never saw the man who attempted to rape me when I was fourteen, again. But in 2015, during a visit home, I learned he'd been hired back, working around children in the same organization where he attempted to rape me and assaulted at least two other girls so many years before. In fact, he'd been back for at least a decade. I contacted another woman who had been assaulted by him as a child, and we spent several months of 2016 attempting to have him removed, *again*, from the same job he was apparently quietly hired back to, repeatedly.

This was a difficult process, and even at the age of thirty-four, I still felt like I was the one who was guilty of something when telling people from this small-town community-theater organization what happened to me years ago. People defend him because they like him. They think of him as a nice guy who's just struggling with a drinking problem. This was true when I was young, and it's true now. The other woman and I received tepid responses from the administration of the organization, saying they were "taking our accusations seriously" and were "looking into it."

Several months passed after we first contacted them, and when we reached out a second time, the administration official we had been in touch with initially ceased responding to our emails and phone calls completely. I inquired with others I knew who were connected to the organization. They said whatever was being done, if anything, was being done quietly. He was still working there.

The other woman and I finally had to go to the authorities to get any response. We called the state Department of Children and Family Services. I found out that because what happened to me was never reported to the police, the statute of limitations had long run out, and there was no way for me to ever have any record of this attack on any books, even though it was an attempted rape of a child. I did not know that attempted child rape had a statute of limitations. Still, through the administration of children's services, we were able to spur an investigation, since there was reason to believe he may still be endangering children. The state administration began an investigation, though they were not legally allowed to report anything back to me regarding the investigation.

I heard through the local grapevine that, as a result of this investigation, he was fired again. All of this is something I did mostly in secret in 2016, that took nearly a year, several hours of emails and phone calls, and recounting my story again and again, in writing and over the phone. This was emotionally difficult for me. But I am proud of myself, and I am proud of this other woman who was assaulted by him as a teenager, for taking the time to do this. We did this because we both know that if he has access to young girls, he will do this again and again. I hoped, after this, that he would not have access to young girls, anymore.

Unfortunately, on another visit home, talking to many people about this, I learned that he was not actually fired, but that he'd simply quit in the middle of the investigation, and so, the investigation was never completed. So he technically could go back to that job in a couple of years, and if there are different people working there who aren't familiar with what happened (most people aren't because this sort of thing is so often handled privately) he could be hired back. I also learned through a grapevine of women in the area that his partner, whom he lives with, runs a day care out of her home and has young daughters. This was all quite disturbing.

During all of this, I made contact with a woman who knew him years before, who told me she'd been raped by him around the same time he sexually assaulted me. She'd never reported it, either, and the statute of limitations has run out for her, too. There is still no official record of this man committing any of these violent crimes against young girls and women, and I have done everything I can at this point to ensure he cannot do this to another person, but it's still not enough, is it?

19

When I was fourteen, I broke up with my sixteen-year-old boyfriend, whom I'd been dating for just over a year. We'd lost our virginity to one another, which many kids in my school and adults in my small town knew. Gossip travels fast in small towns. My boyfriend took the breakup very hard. He told friends he wanted to kill himself. He said things to me that implied he thought it would be better if we both died. Some people were upset with me for breaking up with him. I was told by several peers that I should get back together with him, because he loved me and I was breaking his heart.

After I broke up with him, he continued approaching me in the hallway at school between classes and touching me affectionately, telling me how beautiful I was, and asking me to go out with him again. I repeatedly told him I didn't want to get back together with him.

One day, in the hallway, I was standing and chatting with my best female friend, and he came up to me, pinched my waist, and then put his hand up under my shirt and rubbed the bare skin of my lower back intimately. I grimaced and pulled away from him. He said, "Hey cutie," and winked at me. I sighed and shook my head. He left to go to class. I was shaking with anger. I felt helpless and weak. I didn't want him to touch me that way anymore, and he was doing it constantly, sometimes several times a day, at school. "He won't stop," I lamented to my best friend. "It makes me feel sick to my stomach when he does that."

My friend was angry. She was protective of me. She took me by the arm and said that we were going to go tell the principal. I planted my feet. "He's not really doing anything wrong," I told her. "I just want him to stop acting like we're still together." I didn't want to tell the principal. I didn't want to get him in trouble. What he was doing did not register to me as harassment, though it did make me feel panicked and disgusted.

My best friend was a country girl, an athlete who was never very political, and I don't think anyone would have thought of her as a feminist, but she simply said, "Do you want him touching you like that?" I shook my head no. "Then he has to stop," she said. "If you won't tell the principal, I will."

The principal had been in the room when I'd described the attempted rape by the lighting technician only months before. Even my best friend didn't know about this. I felt guilty going to Mr. Smith with yet another issue about a male touching me sexually without my consent. I thought he would see me as the common denominator in the equation, that he'd see *me* as the problem.

I followed meekly behind my friend, my head down, and she found the principal standing outside his office. She told him that my ex-boyfriend had been touching me romantically all the time, pinching my waist, rubbing me, and that I'd told him to stop, but he kept doing it.

"Is that true?" Mr. Smith asked me.

I looked at my feet and mumbled, "Yeah, but he's just used to touching me that way because he was my boyfriend. He's confused because it used to be okay for him to do that."

The principal was visibly angry. His face reddened. His nostrils flared. He said sternly, "But he's *not* your boyfriend anymore, and if you don't want him to touch you, he can't touch you."

I was shocked by this. I hadn't really thought of it that way, and I definitely didn't think my male principal would see it this way so clearly.

A few hours later, my ex-boyfriend was removed from the school building because he freaked out in class and threw his desk at a female teacher. I was told that Mr. Smith had taken him into his office and had a talk with him about touching me. It was just a short talking-to. He didn't even get in serious trouble, no detention or anything. And I hadn't wanted him to get in serious trouble, either. But after this talk with the principal, he was so upset that he went back to class, sat, and fumed quietly. Then, when the teacher gave him an instruction to participate in the day's activity, he stood up, began yelling at her, picked up his desk, and threw it at her.

He'd always been a good student and had never been violent before. He got some minimal punishment for throwing his desk at the teacher. I believe he had to meet with the guidance counselor for a period and received three days of suspension. Everyone knew he was having a hard time with our breakup, which was why he was acting out, and people felt sorry for him.

A few days after this incident, and about three weeks after I'd broken up with him, I was alone in my house, and I came out of the shower wearing nothing but a towel wrapped around me to find him standing in my kitchen. I'd never been afraid of him before, but in this moment, I was afraid. He was upset about my going to the principal. He said, "Do you know how that felt when he told me 'you better leave that little girl alone,' like I'm some kind of monster?" He berated me for telling on him, and then begged me to come back to him and be his girlfriend again, and when I refused, he screamed at me, called me names, shook his fist at me, banged it on the kitchen table, and told me he wanted to die.

My grandparents finally came home, interrupting his tirade, and he left.

This incident was to become one of a several-years-long string of many similar unannounced visits.

About a month after I broke up with him, I'd missed the school bus, and a boy I knew casually from band practice offered to give me a ride home. I accepted. This boy was a bit of a show-off. He had a metallic purple truck with hydraulics, and on the way home, he took me on a short joyride, the hydraulics bouncing up and down and some ridiculous hip-hop blasting on the speakers. People noticed this, and someone told my ex-boyfriend that I'd been riding around town with this boy. The next day, I got a call from the boy who'd driven me home, saying that my ex had come into his house wielding a knife, shoved him against the wall, and told him that if he ever spoke to me again, he'd kill him. This boy asked me to please tell my ex that he and I were just friends and weren't dating.

I told an adult male family member about everything that was happening, and he responded to me by saying, "Yeah, rejection burns, babe. He's really in love with you. I remember the first time a girl I loved rejected me. It's the worst feeling in the world."

Most people felt sorry for him, and if I talked to them about what was happening, I ended up feeling like the guilty party. I learned to handle the situation, for years. I learned to handle him when he showed up at my house. By the time I was seventeen, my grandma was even used to it. I remember one night, I was in the living room, and the doorbell rang. My grandma went to answer the door, then came and got me, simply saying, "You-know-who is here. I guess you better go deal with it," throwing her hands up and shaking her head. She'd always really liked him, but this did try her patience.

From the time I was fourteen until I moved out, and even after, when I came home to visit, it became almost expected that this boy would show up on my porch in the middle of the night or let himself into my house in the middle of the day and beg me to get back together with him, though, after the first year, his visits lost their threatening edge. The last time he did this, I was twenty-four years old, visiting home from New York City, so I guess this went on for ten years— *ten* years after I broke up with him when I was fourteen.

When I was in my mid-twenties, I was visiting home and stopped by a local diner where my grandfather often sat and had endless cups of coffee with a group of other old men from my town. One of the old men asked me if I'd seen my ex-boyfriend since I was back. (He referred to him by name.) I told him I hadn't. "Well maybe you should stop by and say hi to him," he told me. "That boy sure does like you. I think he wanted to marry you."

There were many implications here. For one, the man most likely knew I'd come out as a lesbian, and was showing his disapproval of that, but also, he was saying that he knew I'd had sex with "that boy," and the right thing for me to do would be to marry him.

In my hometown, when I was younger, in the mid-'90s and early 2000s, this was the pervasive mentality haunting most girls who had serious and sexual relationships with boys in their teens. The general feeling was that if you weren't a slut, and had sex with a boy, that boy basically owned you. I saw many boys react aggressively and violently to being broken up with and rejected by girls, and it was thought of and reacted to as normal behavior for teenage boys. What else did we expect them to do?

My ex-boyfriend actually grew up to be a good person. This may seem crazy to some readers, but we get along now. I enjoy his company. We still have many mutual friends, and when I go home to visit my very small hometown, I am often in the same space as him, and we hang out. I actually like him now, and consider him a casual old friend. He grew up to be a thoughtful, peculiar, and kind person.

From what I know of him now, he is a good person. It seems, from the little interaction I have with him now, that he has honestly matured and changed. But I wonder if things have changed for the teenage girls and boys who are currently growing up in my hometown. I wonder what is still expected of teenage boys. His behavior as a young man after being rejected by a girl was not only allowed, it was expected of him. Is it still normal for boys to have a feeling of eternal ownership over girls they have sex with? Are boys still forgiven for lashing out violently when faced with female rejection? Are young girls still expected to dutifully tend to the hearts they have broken, even if that tending makes them feel they are in danger?

I also often wonder how people would have reacted if the situation were reversed, if he'd broken up with me and I'd reacted the same way he did. How would they have responded to a teenage girl begging her ex-boyfriend to get back together with her, touching him sexually in the hallway, breaking into his house, threatening other girls, attacking a teacher?

While he was seen as "that poor boy" having trouble dealing with a broken heart, I have no doubt I would have been dealt with as a crazy bitch. There are horror movies about women behaving this way. There are romantic comedies about men doing the same.

20

When I was fourteen, I was walking with my dad
to a They Might Be Giants concert at Mississippi Nights
(a music club in Saint Louis). We passed a party bus full of
men, a bachelor party. The men hung out of the windows of
the bus and started yelling flirtatious things at me and whistling. My father stepped between me and the bus and yelled
back at them, "Hey, that's my daughter. She's only fourteen."

One of the men responded by saying, "Well, she can suck
my dick good then." My dad lost his shit, as they say.

21

When I was fifteen, my male PE teacher only allowed the girls to use the dilapidated, old weights and benches, some of which were duct-taped together, while the boys used the nice new benches, weights, and exercise machines. Except for weight lifting, PE was a coed class. When it came to weight lifting, the teacher sent the girls to the other side of the weight room with the old crappy weights. He paid no attention to us while teaching the boys weight-lifting techniques. This upset me, and I made a big issue of it in class, for several days, and the teacher finally said any girl who could bench-press eighty pounds (I believe this was the weight he set, though it was many years ago) would be allowed to take part in the class with the boys.

There were some boys who couldn't bench-press eighty pounds, but they were included in the "real class" and could use the good machines, regardless. This, though, is how I started lifting weights. I did get to his goal, and before the end of the year, was allowed to actually be taught in my PE class, like the boys. But I was the only girl who was granted the privilege of a somewhat equal education in that class.

22

When I was sixteen, I was at a party I definitely shouldn't have been at. I was too drunk and I left the crowd and went into another room to sleep on the couch. I was admittedly so drunk the room was spinning. A boy I had met that night came in and chatted with me briefly. Then, as I was falling asleep, he got on top of me and attempted to rape me.

He held me down with his arm laid flat across my chest, his weight resting on that arm. There was a struggle, which involved my earring actually getting ripped out through the skin of my ear and causing it to bleed. He got my pants and underwear down to my knees and forcibly penetrated me with his hand, making a weird comment, telling me he was fucking me like a lesbian.

He sat up and began unbuttoning his pants, and somehow, in that moment, I was able to lift my legs, and get my feet onto his shoulders. I think he thought I was suddenly consenting, even though I was crying and telling him to stop. I pushed hard with my feet and flipped him backward off the couch, and he hit his head on the wall and then slowly left.

Fifteen years later, a young male relative of mine (who had ended up in jail for a few days) met this boy (now a man) who'd tried to rape me, in the jail, and told me I had come up in conversation. This guy said he knew me and told my relative to say hello to me for him. This guy who tried to rape me when we were both teenagers told him that we had "spent a night" together once when we were younger. He'd clearly implied that we had had sex and seemed to think I had a good time. I thought that was a strange thing to say since neither of these things had happened. I wasn't sure if he actually thought of that event as us spending a night together, or if he was trying to rattle me all those years later. I did feel comforted by the fact that this message was being delivered to me from inside a jail.

Still, his message impacted me deeply. I hated that he had told a younger male relative this, and I felt compelled to tell my relative that the guy had actually assaulted and tried to rape me. I never "spent a night" with him. I really never wanted to say anything about this to my young male relative, and his response was silence, which was probably a result of his shock. When I relate an incident like this to a man, I often fear that I'm not being believed, and I don't know what to make of the listener's silence. I always wonder if they're thinking maybe I had a bad time, or felt ashamed of the sex after and decided to call it rape. I'm not the kind of woman who is ashamed of having spent a night with someone. That is not what happened here.

After I got off the phone with my relative, I felt . . . strange. I hung up and tried to stand from the chair I was sitting in, and I felt a sudden, sharp pain shoot down my back. It was so odd. My back had completely locked up. I didn't feel noticeably or extremely emotionally upset, but my body had reacted for me. I ended up spending three hours in bed, physically unable to walk, because my back went out. It was a strange experience of an intensely physical psychosomatic reaction that I don't totally understand, but I think that hearing a surprise hello from someone who attempted to rape me, delivered through a family member, even fifteen years later, was more upsetting than I could allow myself to fully feel.

23

I was sixteen, and for two years I'd been having sharp pains in my chest sporadically, which coincided with my becoming intensely dizzy. I'd talked about this with my primary physician several times during regular checkups, and he always brushed my comments aside, sometimes implying that I was exaggerating my pain, or that my pain was "in my head." At sixteen, I went through a period where the chest pains became more intense and frequent, and I scheduled an appointment with my physician specifically because of these pains and told him that I was sure I was having some sort of issue with my heart.

My doctor was actually visibly annoyed with me during this visit. He explained to me, as if this was a tedious task, that girls my age have a lot of "pains they don't understand," and he asked me if I understood what my menstrual cycle was. I told him I did, but he still gave me a long explanation of the workings of my menstrual cycle and told me that I was probably confusing menstrual pains with heart issues.

I insisted I knew the difference between chest pains and menstrual cramps. I'd been having my period since I was thirteen, every month, so I was familiar with that type of pain. He admonished me for my insistence that I had a heart problem, telling me that he was going to have to do many expensive tests that my insurance was going to have to pay for. "It's going to cost them a lot of money, probably for nothing," he told me. I was adamant. My paternal grandma (who I had lived with all of my life) also advocated for me, telling the doctor she'd seen me experience this pain, become dizzy and disoriented, and also thought it might be my heart.

So, after a series of "expensive tests" including an electrocardiogram (EKG), a machine I wore for three days that recorded my cardiac activity, and a sonogram, he discovered that I did indeed have a heart problem. I was sent to a cardiologist in the city an hour away, and put on medication for my heart problem. I had an arrhythmia and a prolapsed valve in my heart. This was a genetic condition that was supposed to cause fewer problems as I got older. It was most likely not deadly, but, yes, it sometimes would cause sharp pains, fatigue, the feeling of a racing heart, dizziness, and even unconsciousness, which were all things I'd repeatedly told my doctor I was experiencing. When we were with the cardiologist, and he was listing the symptoms, my grandma told him that she also sometimes experienced these feelings. She said she thought it was probably nothing, but she did wonder if she might have the same issue. The cardiologist, thankfully, took her seriously. He told us that this condition was hereditary, so anyone in the family who experienced similar symptoms to me should be tested. My grandmother went through a similar series of tests, and, yes, she had the same heart issue.

Looking back, it disturbs me to think that my grandma, who I love so immensely and want to live as long a life as possible, may have never spoken up about this because she didn't want to be a bother. I wonder if she had perhaps told her doctor about these symptoms, but had her concerns brushed aside the same way I did.

This problem with doctors didn't stop there. I've found that my main challenge to receiving quality health care has been convincing my doctor I'm not crazy or imagining things. This is true with male and female doctors and is something I've heard from so many women. Our main challenge, when we have a health issue, is convincing the doctor that our pain is a real, physical issue and not "in our heads."

24

When I was seventeen, I was walking alone in Belleville, Illinois from my parked car to my LGBT youth group. A group of five boys who seemed to be around my age were walking behind me. They walked up quickly and surrounded me and started making comments about my breasts. "Hey, what's your name?" they asked. "Are you freaky? You look freaky." (I had a shaved head and dressed punk at that age.) "You have some nice tits. You have some big tits. Can we titty-fuck you? Have you ever been titty-fucked? Would you let all of us titty-fuck you?" They had me surrounded and were lobbing these comments at me all at once.

Sometimes they would block my path and come to a standstill, and I would have to push my way through them to keep walking forward as they kept repeating their absurd questions. They walked with me this way for five blocks on an empty residential street, keeping me encircled. I was terrified. I kept thinking that at any moment they could drag me behind a house or into some cluster of trees and gang-rape me. I finally saw a group of people standing outside the LGBT center a block away. I yelled for them, and the boys ran away.

25

When I was seventeen, a boy who'd graduated
from my school a year earlier, at the age of nineteen, killed
himself and his two-year-old daughter, in retaliation for his
ex-wife and child's mother (who was only eighteen years old)
breaking up with him and getting a new boyfriend.

His ex-wife was a senior in my school when this happened.
She was just one year ahead of me, and had already been
married, was filing for a divorce, and had lost her daughter
just a month before her own high school graduation. She was
absolutely devastated by the murder of her daughter. This was
an intensely sad time in my town. The boy had been a popular
athlete, well-liked by his teachers and many of his peers. I
knew him well enough, though we weren't close. He'd always
been nice to me, but he'd been quite aggressive with a friend
of mine years before, after she rejected his requests to go on a
date with him. Still, the idea that he would ever go so far as to
murder his child and kill himself because of female rejection
was shocking, to say the least.

His ex-wife said that he'd killed their daughter because he
knew this is what would hurt her the most, and he wanted
revenge for her getting with another man. This was more
than speculation on her part. He'd been granted limited custody of the two-year-old girl, weekends only, though it was a

temporary ruling, in place until the custody trial was finalized. In his suicide note, he stated that he loved his daughter, but could not tolerate his daughter living with his ex-wife and another man.

Generally, people felt sorry for his young ex-wife, and devastated over his death and the murder of the baby girl. But there was also another layer to the sentiments of kids in my school. When boys who'd been his friends talked about the murder/suicide, they would say things like, "He couldn't stand the thought of her shacking up with that other guy," and "He couldn't take imagining her raising his baby with that guy. He always wanted a family of his own. He would have been a good husband and father if she'd let him."

I felt uneasy when people talked this way. It seemed like they were implying some level of guilt on his eighteen-year-old ex-wife's part. I hope that no one ever talked that way to her. I hope she didn't feel responsible.

A year later, when I was a senior in high school, somehow word got out that I was dating a black girl who lived in St. Louis, which was a two-hour drive from my town, and was where I spent most of my weekends and summers as a teenager.

The younger brother of the boy who'd killed himself and his two-year-old daughter was my age, and we had many classes together. He confronted me publicly about the fact that I was dating a black girl, calling me a "nigger-lover" and threatening to beat me up. He said I was "a faggot dating an ape," and said something about faggot apes getting AIDS. We got in a physical tussle, shoving each other back and forth in class.

This short fight was quickly broken up by a teacher walking in. I remember feeling shocked at what he'd called me. This was the year 2000, and I thought that particular phrase had been left behind in the 1950s or was relegated to the South, or both. I perhaps had heard it before, in bad jokes the boys told on the bus, or in movies, but never heard it actually directed at anyone. Sure, I heard the N-word all the time, in school, and in bars and at the park, wherever, but this particular phrase, "nigger-lover," seemed dated to me, and it was hard to believe he'd said it. A lot of the things this boy said to me after that were hard for me to believe were really happening.

He continued using that phrase often, and added in words like "faggot," "cunt," "dirty bitch," "nigger-loving faggot" (never "dyke," I don't know why). I verbally stuck up for myself and jabbed him back with my wit, saying, "I'm surprised you have thumbs. You don't believe in evolution, and you're actually starting to make me wonder if it's real, too." My other classmates laugh at him. Standing up for myself was the sort of thing everyone had always told me would defuse situations with bullies, but he began threatening, in earnest, to kill me.

For nearly two months, in every home economics class, which thankfully only occurred twice a week, he took a seat next to me and whispered to me the details of how he planned to kill me. I still remember some of his words exactly.

He said, "What if I stabbed you in the eye with this pen right now and jabbed it around a little to see what your brains are made of? Do you think faggot brains look the same as everyone else's?" He held the pen like a knife and made jabbing motions at me.

He told me that there was nothing I could do about it. That one day I was going to be late getting out of school, and he was going to be there by my car, waiting with a knife or gun. He was going to kill my "faggot ass," stab me in the guts, shoot me in the head, and leave me to die bleeding in the parking lot. No one would know who did it and no one would care to find out because, of course, I was a faggot.

I didn't go to my family with this, because some of them,

at the time, also hated that I was gay, and I didn't want to bring attention to that. In retrospect, I probably could have told my family, but as a teenager who was only partially out and afraid of rejection, that felt too exposing.

I took this boy's threats extremely seriously because of his family history. I wondered if he was as surprisingly capable of serious violence as his brother. On the flip side, this boy who was threatening to kill me was also well-liked, an athlete, and seen as a victim of a horrible tragedy. People felt sorry for him. By the second week of his threats, I found myself visibly trembling in the hallways, terrified for my life. I finally went to the high school principal and made him aware of the situation.

By this time, Mr. Smith, the principal who'd been supportive of me years before, was no longer working at my school. We had a different principal. This one took the phrase, "He's threatening to kill me," with a grain of salt, like I was exaggerating some normal high school spat.

When he asked me, "*Why* is he threatening to kill you?" and I told him, "Because I'm gay and I'm dating a black girl and he doesn't like it," the principal's face dropped. He grew stone-cold, quiet. And then he did something strange. He asked me the question again, as if he hadn't heard what I said at all.

The look on his face actually led me to believe his brain may have literally not processed that I'd actually said what I'd said, and had just reset itself. "*Why* is he threatening to kill you?"

I repeated, hesitantly, meekly, "I think it's because . . . I'm . . . *gay*? And also . . . the girl I'm dating is . . . *black*? That's what he says anyway."

"He's calling you gay?" The principal asked.

"Umm . . . well. I *am* gay. And . . . that's why he's threatening me."

(Long pause) "Okay. Well thanks for letting me know that

you're gay," he said, a lilt in his voice that seemed to me to imply he thought that the point of the meeting had been just for me to come out as gay to him and he found it unnecessary, possibly inappropriate, melodramatic, and annoying. And that was it.

I was sent back to class. Nothing was done. The detailed, in-person death threats continued to be a weekly part of my high school education.

Later that week, I confided in one of the few teachers I trusted, a female science teacher. She took it upon herself to begin escorting me to my car every day, which, in retrospect would have probably been no help if he decided to try to kill me. She probably couldn't have protected me or herself physically from this young man. At the time, though, having an adult with me made me feel safe, and without that teacher, I may have stopped going to school altogether.

His threats finally ended, because about a month after I went to the principal, this boy physically attacked a male teacher. He was put on a long suspension and was ordered to go into anger management counseling. Because of this incident, he began taking most classes separate from the rest of the students.

I was so relieved he was gone. When he attacked that male teacher everyone acted shocked, even though so many people knew he had been threatening to kill me for quite a while.

26

When I was eighteen, I got a job in St. Louis working for a new pizza restaurant that was two weeks away from opening. The owner was a man in his mid-fifties who was starting the restaurant with his wife, but she was almost never around. He only hired girls between the ages of seventeen and twenty-three to work there. I worked there for three days with about twelve other girls. But he hadn't really "hired" us technically. He interviewed us, told us all that we had the job, and then put us to work. He never told us how much we would be paid or had us fill out any forms, or gathered any relevant information from us that's typical for a business with a payroll. I kept asking him when I was supposed to fill out my tax forms and get an actual contract and when he was going to tell us exactly how much we would be paid.

He kept saying that he would pay us after the restaurant opened in two weeks, and we would be compensated for the work we were doing helping him open it. We were cleaning up the kitchen, setting up the tables and chairs, stocking food and supplies, and painting the interior of the restaurant. This was physical labor with no contract and no set pay rate or pay schedule.

The other girls seemed to trust him completely and had no issue with this. I wanted to have my name on the books and to have an actual salary set in a contract, as I'd always done before when I was hired somewhere.

Throughout the process, he would often have us all come into his office for long meetings, where we would sit in a circle in a small space with him. The meetings were mostly him telling us about his past successes and assigning us little nicknames. He said my nickname was Red.

He always sat in the middle of any given two girls, very close to them, and would touch the girls a lot. He smacked one girl on her inner thigh a couple of times while he was joking around during his meeting. She was wearing shorts, so he was smacking her bare skin and sometimes, he would rest his hand on a girl's bare leg while he talked. He smacked another girl's ass as she was leaving his office, right in front of all of us. The girl laughed it off. The most he did with me was put his arm around me and caress my shoulder a few times, and he tried to hold my hand, but I was standoffish. I would lean away or make an excuse to get away when he did this sort of thing and made sure never to sit next to him in a meeting.

I started getting on his nerves because I would not stop asking, while we were working and in front of the other girls, how much we were getting paid an hour and when we were going to sign our contracts. When I got no answer from him after the third day, I stopped going in. I gave him three days of free labor. I don't know how much longer the other girls endured this free labor job, where the only "perk" was sexual harassment. I never bought a slice of pizza there.

27

When I was nineteen, in Saint Louis, I was walking home alone at night, and suddenly became aware a man was following me. I crossed the street to get away from him, hoping that he wasn't actually following me, but just happened to be walking closely behind me. When I did this, he crossed the street too, keeping in stride, very close to me. I was sure he was following me, so I began running, and then he began running, and then I realized I was actually running for my life.

He chased me at full speed, sometimes nearly catching up with me, at which point he would lunge and try to grab me. He chased me for ten blocks, even turning with me down different streets, until finally, I made it to a heavily trafficked road and ran out into the middle of the street, waving my hands into the headlights of cars. When the cars stopped, I turned to where he had been, and he was gone.

28

When I was nineteen, an older man I knew well,
who I was friends with, who was a writer and part of the
literary scene (he ran a reading series) invited me over to his
house to read and workshop poetry, which I gladly accepted.

We read poetry and had some drinks and snacks. He asked
me if I wanted to watch *1984*. I loved the book but had never
seen the film. We went to the TV room, which didn't have
chairs but rather some big reclining-style pillows and blankets
on the floor. I sat down on the floor next to him, and about
five minutes into the movie, he laid on his back, then rolled
over, grabbed my arm, and tried to pull me down to kiss me. I
guess this was him making a not-so-smooth move.

I pulled away and told him I didn't want to kiss him.
He kept tugging at my arm and tried to roll on top of me
and push me down to a lying position. He was drunk and
an awkward struggle ensued. I finally got him off me and
shouted at him, "I told you, I don't want to." He started
crying and saying, "please." I tried to be nice and give him
a pass, because I was very young and uncertain of myself,
and he was drunk and sad, and my friend. I told him what
he already knew, that I was a lesbian and didn't feel that way
about him, "Now can we please just watch the movie?" If it
had ended there, I wouldn't be writing this right now.

But after a few minutes, he did the whole thing over again. Grabbed my arm, tried to push me down, started trying to kiss me. I shoved him off me and stood. I cussed at him and told him I was leaving. "No, please don't. Give me a chance," he begged from the floor. I told him to cut it out, and turned to leave, and he grabbed me by my ankle and started tugging at it, hard.

I fell over, and he tried to crawl on top of me, but I was able to stand back up before he was able to get on top of me and hold me down, though he still had hold of my ankle with a tight grip. It was hard for me to believe this was actually happening, that he, a close friend, would actually try to physically force me. I knew him well, which is why I had kept trying to de-escalate the situation, but finally, panic took over, and I kicked the foot he had hold of, hard, shaking him off, grabbed my things, and ran out the door.

He called and left me several apologetic messages the next day. I didn't see how I could participate in the poetry scene without being cool with him, so I let it go and remained friendly with him. Though I made sure to never be alone with him again.

29

When I was nineteen, my supervisor at work repeatedly asked me to have a threesome with him and his wife.
If he'd done this only once, and taken my no for an answer,
I wouldn't be including this in the book. But he asked me
several times, after I made it clear I wasn't interested. He was
in his mid-twenties and funny and cool, and I liked him a
lot, and even looked up to him. But he also constantly made
me feel demeaned, commenting on my body in front of my
coworkers, asking me if I'd gained or lost weight regularly,
and even commenting on the shape and size of my breasts.

Men my age also worked the same job I did and got
promoted quickly. I was one of the top-ranking employees in
my position, as far as actual sales were concerned, but I was
never offered a raise or promotion and never even thought
to ask. Only men held any positions above the one I was in,
and it was clear to me that wasn't my place. My supervisor
asking me to have sex with him regularly and commenting
on my body didn't really make me think my skills as an
employee were valued in any serious way.

The day I quit, he thanked me for my work and told me
he would provide a good reference for me. Then he asked
me to come into the storage closet with him. I thought he
was going to give me a parting gift, but instead, he closed

the door behind us, and said, "Okay, now that I'm not your boss, would you have a threesome with me and my wife?" I grimaced and told him no, calmly and sadly. He said, "Well, can't hurt to ask."

30

When I was twenty, still living in Saint Louis, two of
my female lovers and one of my close gay male friends were all
raped in the same year, two by strangers, and one by someone
we knew. This didn't happen to me, but going through this
repeatedly with three unrelated people I was deeply intimate
with in such a short time changed me forever.

One of my lovers was hospitalized and had to have
stitches in the places where the man who assaulted her had
bitten out chunks of her flesh. She was a butch lesbian, and
it was strange and painful seeing someone who seemed to be
so strong and beautiful become so helpless. To me, she was
the strongest, hottest, butchest girl in the Midwest. When
she was around, I'd always felt safe. I'd never thought of her
as someone who needed protecting. Every dyke wanted to
be with her. She was a stud. The idea that a man could have
rendered her powerless was surreal.

The man was a stranger who had pushed his way into her
house as she was coming home from work. He told the police
he was having an affair with her, and that her boyfriend had
come home and caught them having sex, and chased him
out, and that it must have been her boyfriend who beat her
unconscious, and that she was claiming it was rape for her
boyfriend's benefit, so that he wouldn't get mad at her.

She didn't have a boyfriend. She'd never had a boyfriend. She was a gold-star butch. She was *my* lover, and probably had another girl on the side too. But the police still believed him, somehow.

She was hospitalized for days, and the detectives on the case sympathized with her rapist. While she was in the hospital, one detective on the case even referred to him as "that poor man." Because of this, and after several months of intense emotional discussions with a lawyer and arguments with the detectives, she decided not to go to court and press charges.

When she told me this, I thought, "we're nothing to them." Queer women, that is. We don't exist. They don't see us.

They looked at this hot, fierce butch, and I wondered what they saw—a "larger," plain woman with a short haircut who dressed unassumingly and for some reason needed to pathetically lie about being beaten and raped?

When she got out of the hospital she came and stayed with me, and we didn't leave my bed for two days. It was a blue cocoon. I did my best to comfort her, but I was also young and emotional, and it was difficult in moments for me to give exactly what she needed. I was also hurting and not coping well. I did my best. I hope it is a good memory for her, because for me, those days lying together and holding each other for hours on end are sacred.

I remember her bruises as blue, the room as blue, and the color of the air as blue. I realized, for the first time in our long relationship, that she must've seen me as powerful too if she came to me after that happened to her. I realized we were both powerful together, because we could actually see and value each other. But that time left a blue mark on my heart also, as I realized, after everything that had happened that year, we were really nothing to the cops, nothing to so many straight men . . . nothing to the powers that order the world. Nothing.

31

When I was twenty, I was about three days away
from moving out of the cute little apartment I was living in
on the Hill in Saint Louis, to move in with some friends of
mine in a different neighborhood. It was around eight in the
morning. It was summer. I was totally alone in my apartment, and was sleeping naked, on top of the covers, in my
bed, in my bedroom, in the back of the apartment. I woke to
find a man I didn't recognize standing over my bed, staring
at me.

He was a well-dressed man in his early sixties. I didn't
know how long he'd been standing there, staring at me
while I was naked and asleep. I started and screamed. "Don't
worry," he said, calmly, holding out his hand. "It's me.
Your landlord. It's the landlord," he repeated, as if this were
somehow reassuring.

I stared at him. I was still totally naked, but was now
sitting up with my back against the headboard. He smiled
at me and looked me up and down, and sighed heavily, a
smile lighting his face, like he was taking in a beautiful sight.
I grabbed the blankets and pulled them up, covering myself.
I suddenly recognized him. He was, in fact, my landlord, a
man I'd met once, a year before.

"I just came to see how the move out was going," he said.

"Do you need any help?" I shook my head no. "Okay, well, what date *will* you be out?" He asked me this with an incredulous tone, like I was doing something wrong.

"The thirtieth!" I screamed. "I *live* here till the *thirtieth*! Next week!"

"Okay, okay. Calm down. Go back to sleep. I didn't mean to disturb you." He smiled and stared at me harder. He stepped forward and held out his hand to me again, weirdly. I pulled the covers tighter. "I'm the landlord," he repeated, then smiled, nodded, and left.

I called the police.

32

I called the police on my landlord for breaking into my apartment and watching me sleep naked in my bed. One male officer came and interviewed me. He refused to file a report and said it was a civil matter. He was gross about the whole thing.

He literally chuckled the whole time and asked me, "Exactly how naked are we talking? Like underwear?" (Chuckle, chuckle.)

No. No underwear.

Still giggling like a kid, he asked, "Okay, okay." (Deep breath to stop chuckling.) "Okay. Is this guy black?" He was trying to get serious, I guess.

No.

"Is he a foreigner?" I asked why that mattered, and the cop explained to me, "Foreigners have different ideas about nudity. Most landlords here are foreign. He probably didn't even think of it as sexual, like we do."

He told me what my landlord had done wasn't breaking and entering, since he owned the property. That I could take this to a civil court, but he wouldn't be able to file a report because there were no charges to be pressed.

33

When I was twenty, I was reading a poem at an open mic in Saint Louis. At this point in my life I really felt frayed because of all of these experiences (and some others having to do with my class and sexuality). I was a live wire, blowing in the wind, giving off sparks.

I was at an open mic, standing on stage, reciting a poem I'd written about the childhood rape of a close female family member, which then went on to extend this experience to all women and society at large. It was an intense poem about rape and systemic sexism. At the same time that two women started snapping, nodding "yes," and verbally supporting my piece, one with tears in her eyes, several men started moaning, and one started screaming at me.

He was older than me, in his fifties, and while I was in the middle of the poem, he screamed at me to "Shut up!" I kept going. Then, this man (an audience member and poet) actually jumped up onto the stage and grabbed the microphone out of my hand.

I stood facing him and finished the poem, screaming it loudly, directed at him, as he stood holding the mic and glaring at me. I was trembling and shouting with tears rolling down my cheeks. Honestly, I wanted to kill him and I knew he wanted to kill me too.

34

I was twenty-one, living in Saint Louis. Several months after two of my lovers and one of my close friends were all raped within a few weeks of each other, one of my lovers, who had been raped by someone we knew, told me the man who raped her had started stalking her.

He was showing up to her performances, sitting and watching her, and then leaving before she was done with her sets, so she couldn't confront him without doing it publicly.

Though this woman and I had broken up months before, we were still close, and one time when he showed up at her performance, I was there. I was standing outside the venue with a lot of people right before the show started. He walked up as though everything was normal. As soon as I saw him, all I could think about was the bat that my lover had started keeping right next to our bed as she slept. She had slept with that bat next to the bed every night since it had happened. The aftermath of her rape had completely destroyed our relationship. It made both of us markedly different people. It felt like my insides were on fire when I saw him approaching, and as soon as he was near me I attacked him.

I did this outside a busy venue, in the daytime, in front of many people dressed up for a show, some of whom I knew well, and many whom I'd never met. I ran up to him and started hitting him repeatedly and screaming, and people had to pull me off of him. After they pulled me away, they let me go, and I attacked him a second time, and then he ran away. After that, something had changed in me. Something had deeply snapped.

35

I was twenty-one, and had just moved to New York City. I hosted a daylong music and poetry event for A Gathering of the Tribes, a multicultural salon-style gallery and performance space in New York City where I lived for two years and worked for six years. The DJ for the event was a man possibly in his late thirties. He was married with kids. I had met him for the first time that day. Earlier in the day, his kids had been present, but by the time the event was over, they were gone. When the event was over, we hung out with a crowd of people in the gallery and were being friendly, chatting and having a glass of wine because we'd just worked together for several hours.

He thanked me for doing such a good job as a host, and told me I was beautiful. This was awkward. I just nodded and mumbled, "Oh okay, thanks." Then, he grabbed me and smashed me against the wall and stuck his tongue in my mouth. I didn't really know what to do. I was still young and sometimes uncertain of myself. He was four times my size, and he forcibly kissed me for a long time. When he let me go, I just walked away in silence, feeling confused.

After that, every time I saw him, for the next year, he gave me intense hugs and held me too long and too tight, rubbing my back and hips, and made me feel generally gross.

Then, at a gallery opening where he was volunteering, he grabbed a young female intern's thigh. This girl was my age, and was a feminist who attended Sarah Lawrence College. She was sitting next to him while they were working the wine table together. She was wearing a short skirt and while chatting with her, he grabbed her bare thigh and squeezed it. Without missing a beat, she dumped her glass of wine over his head in front of everyone. All the people in the room glared at him. Most of us had seen what he'd done. He left the gallery covered in wine and in shame. This incident emboldened me. The next time he tried to hug me, I wouldn't let him. I made it clear that he was never to hug me again. In fact, I wouldn't even shake his hand. I still see him around town sometimes, hanging out with groups of people I know, and even after all these years, I still won't do more than nod a hello when I see him. I think he thinks I'm a bitch now. Fine.

36

When I was twenty-one, there was a male poet in his mid-forties who attended nearly every reading I went to in downtown New York City. (At that age, I frequented multiple open mic and poetry readings every week.)

This man always had a Polaroid camera on him, along with a bag of several large photo albums full of snapshots of women flashing him their tits, mostly taken at poetry events.

The first time I ever went to a poetry open mic in New York City, this man approached me and asked me if he could take a photo of my breasts. "Just lift up your shirt," he coaxed. "I'll even buy you a drink." I refused. He showed me pictures of all of the other women who had done it. I felt deeply uncomfortable with this, and hated that this was one of my first conversations with another poet upon arriving to New York City. At a reading in a venue that's beloved among writers, that I had dreamed about for so many years. But all of the older poets who were embedded in the NYC poetry scene, many of whom I greatly admired, were friendly with this man, seemed to know him well, and treated him like a harmless eccentric, even though he approached all the women he encountered as if our bodies were hunting trophies, pelts he collected and added to his weird photo albums of tits.

For over a year, almost every time I came to any poetry open mic, this man nagged me to lift up my shirt and bra so he could take a photo of my breasts and add it to his collection. I *hated* this. Still, I simply repeatedly said no to his advances and laughed him off like everyone else did.

Sometimes, he would talk to me about things that weren't my breasts, like writing for instance, and I think he thought we were friends. He didn't know I despised him because he was treating me like I was an animal whose hide he wanted to claim. Eventually, after about a year of me saying no, he stopped asking me. I didn't exactly like him, but I was in the same space with him at least once a week, usually more. The open mics had a "drinkie" party atmosphere, and when he finally stopped asking me to flash him all the time, I found a way to enjoy his company.

When I was twenty-two, I was at a big poetry party in Tribeca. It was an annual celebration that was raucous and pulled many writers from around the city. I was still living at the artist space A Gathering of the Tribes in the Lower East Side. I was extremely poor at this time in my life. I had virtually no income and worked in exchange for a free place to live. It was the end of January, excessively cold, and I had admittedly gotten drunk and stayed too late at the poetry event. I was one of the last people left at the venue, except for this man with the Polaroid camera, and I had lost my $20 bill, which was all the money I had to my name that day, which I was going to use for a cab home. Walking that far (Tribeca to the Lower East Side) while intoxicated, in the severe cold, was not an option. This man was there, and knew the situation I was in, because he heard me talking to a friend about it, and he interrupted and told me he was getting a cab going toward the Lower East Side, and that I could ride with him. He said that he would drop me off. I accepted this act, what I thought was simply him being friendly to someone he'd spent time with every week for more than a year, and now knew well.

Once we got in the cab, he told me that his apartment was in a different neighborhood, and that he would only take me back to my neighborhood if I finally let him take a photo of my breasts. He said this in a singsong tone, as if it was funny. He said he *wouldn't* even get my face in the picture, like that was a compromise. He held up the Polaroid camera he always carried with him and smiled. "It's pretty cold out there. You don't want to walk. What's the big deal? Come on. Let me take a picture?" he asked, as the cold lights of the city passed by the window.

37

I was twenty-one, working at A Gathering of the
Tribes. It was a very open, bohemian space where people
came in and out as they pleased throughout the day to view
the art in the gallery, chat with other artists, bang on the
piano, and kind of do whatever they felt like. The space
was generally amazing, and the sometimes wild, liberated
atmosphere that Steve Cannon created was exactly what
I had moved to New York City to be part of. Unfortunately, this level of openness also meant that it was easy for
creeps to come in and take advantage of the situation. A
few young men came in this day, and hung out for several
hours (which was quite normal, and, in fact, encouraged).
One of them, though, was creepy to say the least. He was
pretty young, probably near my age, in his early twenties
and from the moment he saw me, I felt like he was simulta-
neously attracted to me and hated me.

He said weird, intimidating, and not-so-veiled sexual
things to me every time we were in the same room. From his
perspective, he was visiting a cool art space full of strange and
interesting people and I was one of them. But for me, well, I
was at work, running errands for Steve Cannon (the executive
director, who is a blind, retired professor and novelist), and
handling the "business of Tribes." I didn't like this young man

and his agitated advances, and after a couple of disturbing conversations, I completely ignored him, which seemed to piss him off. Finally, he and his friends left.

Steve asked me to go get him a coffee and sandwich. I left to go to the deli, and the creepy dude and his friends were sitting on the stoop of my building smoking. As I walked past them, the creepy guy tried to talk to me and asked me for my number. I declined, trying to be polite because he really freaked me out.

I went to the deli and when I came back, his friends were gone and he was the only one on the steps.

I nodded hello and walked past him. As I did so, he said, "Hey, can I ask you a question?" I stopped on the step above him, and he turned, grabbed my right ankle, and gripped it tightly. I stared at him and he stared back up at me, blankly.

"What are you doing?" I asked.

"Nothing," he responded casually. "What are you doing?"

"Let go of my ankle." I said, sternly, really tired of men grabbing my ankles at this point.

"Why?" he said dryly, sucking on his cigarette, still staring at me, a glint of glee now present in his eyes.

It was the middle of the afternoon on a residential NYC street. I didn't imagine this could go on long without someone walking by. I tugged my leg. His grip tightened. He was strong. "Hey, what's your problem with me anyway?" he asked.

"I said, LET GO OF MY FUCKING ANKLE! FUCKING LET GO! LET GO FUCKING LET GOOOOO!" I was shouting like a crazy person at the top of my lungs and kicking the foot he was holding. I'd completely lost it. He let go quickly, held his hands up, and shouted, "What the hell is your fucking problem?"

I ran up the stairs, slammed the door and locked it, and told Steve no one else was allowed to come in that day.

38

I was twenty-two years old. I was dancing at my favorite NYC bar/café/music venue (Apocalypse) a block away from Tribes, where I was living at the time. I was there with a female friend of mine. We were having a great time. That place played the best music.

There was a man at the bar who kept hitting on me even though I clearly told him no and kept ignoring him. Finally, he followed me out to the dance floor and tried to dance with me. I scooted away from him. He danced up to me and tried to take my hands in his. I pulled away and told him over the music, "No thanks. I don't want to dance." I turned my back and started dancing with my friend, who I was trying to focus on flirting with. She was sometimes a casual lover and we were having a good vibe that night.

Within a minute or two, I felt this man pressing against me from behind, his hands sliding around my waist to my stomach, dancing close and saying "sexy," pulling me into him. I turned slightly, swung my arm around his neck, grabbed onto the wrist of that arm with my other hand, putting him in a choke hold, and lifted both my feet off the ground (I weighed about 110 pounds) to give it some real force. He doubled over. My feet touched the ground and I had him in a headlock. I held him that way for a couple of seconds, then let go and he fell to the floor, to my shock, unconscious. After a second or two, he opened his eyes. I stared at him. He said the strangest thing: "Just like old times." Then he held his hand out for me to help him up and, for some reason, I took it and pulled him to his feet.

Then he looked scared of me, stepped away quickly, and looked me up and down. A few punk queers who were in the bar applauded. (This was a punk bar.) The man went and sat down with his drink at the far end of the bar, and didn't talk to me again. I heard another man tell him, "Damn, that little girl in the miniskirt knocked you out!"

39

The first time I went to a gynecologist, I was twenty-two. I was raised in a conservative, religious environment where I'd long understood that I shouldn't need to go to a gynecologist for a regular Pap smear or gynecological checkup until I was married or had some serious issue, which as a young teenager, I didn't. And when I was an older teen I was queer. The subject of my sexuality and sexual health was a touchy topic and my going to a gynecologist was never brought up. It didn't seem to be something that was "for me," even though I'd been sexually active since I was fourteen.

When I was twenty-two and living in New York City, many of my close friends thought it was insane that I'd never been to a gynecologist and insisted that I needed to have a checkup at least once a year. I didn't have any health insurance, but finally I made an appointment at the sliding-scale health clinic near where I lived in the Lower East Side. I was nervous about my first exam and I specifically requested a female gynecologist, but I was told that the female ob-gyns were booked up for several months, so I accepted an appointment with a male gynecologist.

The ob-gyn was a straight white man in his sixties. I was a weirdly dressed, probably poor-looking punk kid with pink hair. He had me fill out a form and did an intake with me before the exam. He sat across from me with the form I'd filled out in front of him.

"You didn't state what type of birth control you're on. What do you take?" he asked. I told him I didn't take birth control. I never had. He blustered. "You *must* begin taking birth control," he told me. "A girl your age, who has been with as many people as you have, you have to be on birth control."

There was a box on the form where I'd been asked to fill in how many sexual partners I'd had and I had filled that in honestly.

"Oh, no," I told him. "I don't need birth control. I only sleep with women. I'm a lesbian."

His face hardened. He let out a long sigh. "So, all of these," he pointed to the box with my dreaded number scrawled in it, "*all* of these are women?" he asked, incredulous.

"All but one," I responded.

"I see." He folded his arms and leaned back. And then he said—and I remember this word for word because I almost got up and left and should have— he said, "And I hear you've requested a female doctor as well. Why? Is it because you think women do it better?"

At this point, I was extremely uncomfortable. But I was also twenty-two years old, younger than I realized then, new to New York City, living off the grid, didn't have insurance, and this doctor had quickly made me feel like there was something wrong with me. He was older, and confident, and I didn't know where else I could go for health care if I walked out and upset this man. (The clinic had given me an affordable sliding-scale rate because I was uninsured and this was where I saw my primary physician and dentist.)

I told this doctor that I'd never been to an ob-gyn before, was nervous, felt more comfortable with a woman, and that's why I had requested a female gynecologist. But, "No, I don't think women are necessarily better doctors."

He had me take off my clothes, put on a robe and get in the stirrups. He was standing behind a curtain, about four feet away from me, and called a female nurse over, saying loudly and gruffly (though obviously I could hear him quite clearly), "I've got a very nervous patient in there. She's uncomfortable around men. I need you to be in there with me and help keep her calm."

He came in with the nurse, a woman in her late fifties. He took a spot at the seat between my legs and the nurse stood by my head. She took my hand in hers and began patting my shoulder. Then one of the most surreal interactions I've ever had began.

The doctor said, loudly and sharply, to the nurse, "Tell her I'm going to place a lubricant on her vagina and insert one finger."

"He's going to place a lubricant on you and then place one finger in you," the nurse said in a calm sweet voice, as if she were talking to a child.

He examined me with his hand, then said, also loudly, "Tell her I'm now going to place the speculum in her and open it, and she might feel a slight pinching."

This was insane. Clearly I could hear everything he was saying. He was so close he was actually inside my body while he was speaking to me through the nurse, instead of speaking directly to me. The nurse said to me as she patted my shoulder, "He's going to place the speculum in you now, and you might feel . . ."

"I heard him," I said, cutting her off. "He can speak directly to me." I lifted my head and viewed the doctor between my legs. "You can just talk directly to me," I told him. At that moment, he slid the speculum in me and opened it. I gasped slightly and wiggled because it pinched, and he grabbed my shin and shouted "*Easy! Easy!*" He was speaking directly to me, but I felt like he was talking to a horse.

The rest of the exam went as normally as possible with him. He spoke directly to me, though brusquely. When it was over, he had me get dressed and wait in another room. He met with me several minutes later and told me that he had seen a lesion on my cervix, and that while we were going to have to wait for the results of my Pap smear, he was probably going to need to do a biopsy. He said all this like he was mad at me, like I'd done something wrong. "A lesion?" I asked.

"Yes," he said. "Possibly several." He looked down and shook his head, disappointed with me. "It doesn't surprise me, given your sex history."

I got a call the next day saying my Pap smear was "inconclusive" and that the doctor wanted to schedule a cervical biopsy as soon as possible.

I went in for the biopsy the next day. This was an equally uncomfortable and much, much more painful procedure than the exam. It hurt while it was happening and afterward I was sore inside.

I went out with Steve Cannon to a poetry reading that night. While I was sitting next to Steve, I began feeling a horrible pain in my lower abdomen, somewhat similar to menstrual cramps, but sharper. I went to the bathroom and found that I was bleeding, a lot. It wasn't time for my period and the blood looked brighter than menstrual blood. I told Steve, and he took me in a cab to the emergency room at Beth Israel Hospital.

I'd never been to an ob-gyn before, but that night I was examined by three gynecologists, two of them women. I told them what the doctor at the clinic had told me about the lesions, and that I had a biopsy earlier that day. They were concerned about what I told them. None of the ob-gyns at the emergency room saw any sign of lesions on my cervix, but they *did* see where he'd performed a biopsy on me. While they examined me together, they kept giving each other these wide-eyed, knowing looks and shaking their heads, their mouths open, looking shocked. He had "messed up" the biopsy, they finally said. He cut my cervix too deeply, is what I was able to gather, but I also felt that they were trying not to be too detailed to keep from upsetting me. They told me the botched biopsy had caused me to hemorrhage, but it was a minor hemorrhage and they treated me for the biopsy wound. They gave me some medication to take and told me I may feel discomfort for a couple more weeks, but that it would end up healing all right. They also performed a Pap smear in the emergency room, which they tested right there and the results came back normal. Normal! Except for the wound on my cervix from the biopsy, I had a healthy vagina.

One of the female ob-gyns referred me to Callen-Lorde, a queer-centered, feminist health clinic in the West Village. She scheduled a follow-up appointment with an ob-gyn there. Three weeks later I went to an appointment with a queer, female ob-gyn and had a much better experience. I got a Pap smear there as well, just to be on the safe side, since the doctor at the first clinic had told me I had an abnormal Pap. This Pap also came back totally normal.

I was healthy, free of STDs, cancer, and lesions. Four other doctors had confirmed this. Still, two days after I got out of the emergency room, the original horrible doctor had left me a message on my phone saying that the results of my biopsy were also "inconclusive" and he wanted to perform a second biopsy. I never got back to him.

40

At this point in my life, I had no patience when it came to anything sexist, assaultive, or remotely nonconsensual with men. I had no ability left to withhold any anger. I began physically assaulting men, quite often. I was like a feral animal. I looked punk and bizarre. Sometimes I just twisted my hair into a horn that seemed to be growing out of the front of my head. I was living in the Lower East Side, had adopted a bohemian lifestyle and, to top it off, I became an extremely assaultive "feminazi."

If a man came on to me once and I didn't like him, I would tell him clearly that I wasn't interested. If he came on to me a second time or touched me after I'd said no once, often I would hit him. I would smack him, or shove him, or punch him in the arm, or whack him in the head with the soft plastic water bottle I usually had on me. Once (okay, maybe twice), I bit a man's ankles. And I realize that most of the things I was reacting to were things many women would think of as normal male behavior that they could deal with, shrug off, and easily forget. But I simply could not. Not for those couple of years. I was done with men not taking me seriously when I said no. I was done with men saying casually sexist things to me. The lines had been drawn. I felt like I was fighting a war . . . and I was.

One night, for instance, I went out with a group of

friends to a birthday party at a bar. There was a well-spoken, traditionally handsome college guy there who was a few years older than me. He was a friend of a friend and was interested in me. He was a frat guy, not my type even if I'd been into men. Which at that time I was not at all in any way. I kept trying to get away from him at the bar, but he kept following me around. He asked me out on a date repeatedly and I repeatedly said no. I told him I was a lesbian and was not interested in men at all. I told him even if I wasn't a lesbian, he still wouldn't be my type. He bugged me so much, I left the party early.

He followed me out of the bar and asked me once more to let him take me on a date. I told him no, once more, and that I wanted to be left alone, but he insisted on walking me home. I said, "No, I want to walk alone." I started walking and he started walking beside me. I said, "Stop following me."

He laughed and said, "You are so weird, but you're just going to have to deal with it." He was talking to me like I was a small child he was winning over. He continued, "I like you. I think you're gorgeous. I'm going to be a gentleman and walk you home." I hopped to the side, punched him in the back of the head twice, and ran.

"What the fuck? Are you crazy?" he screamed.

Yes.

The next day, my female friend who'd invited me to the party the previous night confronted me. "My friend said you *assaulted* him after you left the party together."

"Yeah, I did. And we didn't leave the party together. I left. He followed me."

She asked if he'd done something to me. I explained again, that I'd told him I didn't want to date him, that I didn't want him to walk me home, and he wouldn't stop following me.

She told me, "He's a really nice guy. You can't hit people for no reason."

"Whatever."

41

I was twenty-two, hanging out in front of the glam rock club I went to every weekend, with a female friend of mine. A guy she was casual friends with was flirting with her and standing with us as we smoked. We were all talking. Somehow, the subject of rape came up (I probably brought it up) and the guy started explaining something to us, which I've heard from men hundreds of times. He told us we couldn't understand what it's like to feel sexually out of control, because men's sex drive, arousal, and sexual pleasure are so much more intense than women's.

I didn't respond verbally but whacked him over on the top of his head with my water bottle. "What the fuck is wrong with you, you crazy bitch?" I whacked him again. (I did this calmly.) This time he ran away.

My friend turned and took me by the shoulders. "You can't do that!" She told me.

"That was really sexist," I responded.

"It's not okay. You can't keep hitting any man who comes on to you twice or says something sexist."

"Why not?" I asked dryly.

42

I was twenty-two, and it was SantaCon. SantaCon is a special time, right before Christmas, when frat boys dress up as Santa Claus and get very drunk and sexually harass people in public.

I was at a pretty queer (though it was mixed), glam rock, Goth dance party in the East Village. I was outside smoking, and a very drunk SantaCon frat boy came up and tried to give me a hug. I stepped back from him and told him, annoyed, "I don't want a hug."

He started laughing and said, "Oh come on, give Santa a hug." He reached out and embraced me, giving me a big hug, lifting me onto my toes.

I shoved him and grabbed the plastic water bottle I always had in my pocket and started whacking him over the head with it. I shoved him again and punched him in the shoulder repeatedly, yelling "I said I didn't want a hug!" He was covering his head, shouting, "What the fuck? Stop it!"

Suddenly, I heard someone shouting my name. I stopped hitting the drunk Santa and turned to see a close friend from Saint Louis standing on the sidewalk, staring at me. I shouted his name, ran up to him, and we embraced. "What the hell are you doing in New York?" I asked him.

"I'm visiting a friend, it was a last-minute trip," he told

me. He motioned to the woman who was holding his arm. I held out my hand to introduce myself. She shook it, but was giving me a weird look. My friend looked back to where the drunk Santa was still recovering. "Umm, were you just beating up Santa?" he asked.

"Oh yeah. I was. He hugged me," I told him with no other explanation. At that point, it was so normal for me to be hitting a man when I was out I didn't even think about it. My friend shrugged and laughed awkwardly. I think he was worried about my sanity.

43

When I was twenty-two, I moved to upstate New York where I lived for nearly one year. Some close friends of mine from New York had also recently moved to the same town. My friend Norman Douglas had been there for a few months before I came. He showed me around the town and took me out to what would become one of my favorite bar/restaurant hangouts. This was a hangout spot frequented by artists, writers, and intellectuals. My friend was also a writer and it was common for people to discuss politics, art, current events, and philosophy.

It was my second or third night in town. The bar was mostly empty. A man who knew my friend Norman casually came up to us. He introduced himself to me, very jovial. Then he turned to my friend and said, "Well, Norman Mailer just blew feminism out of the water." This wasn't a good foot to start off on with me.

Norman Mailer was a celebrated, National Book Award– and Pulitzer Prize–winning novelist and essayist who theorized a lot about how men are oppressed by feminism. He also attempted to murder his wife by stabbing her repeatedly, for which he only served three years' probation, which men who love him never like to talk about.

We had a low-key political debate. This guy went on and

on about everything Norman Mailer had ever said about men, and about men's natural biological behavior, and how straight men are being oppressed in the current society. I also know Norman Mailer thought straight, *white* men are particularly oppressed, but, I noted, this white guy wasn't saying that fully. He'd started to, but blustered and stopped, perhaps, I thought, because my friend Norman is black and he was trying not to offend him.

He actually expected me to agree with his anti-feminist rhetoric for some reason. He thought he was wowing me with his intellect. Norman nodded at him and said "uh huh" and "ahh" in a way that, because I knew him well, I knew meant he thought the guy was a clown. I argued with him a lot, but I don't think he realized how deeply I hated the things he was saying. I *hate* Norman Mailer. Eventually, my friend Norman and I went and sat down at the end of the bar with our beers.

This Norman Mailer fan came over and offered to buy me a drink. I was almost finished with my beer, but I declined. "Oh come on," he said. "Can't a man even buy a woman a drink anymore?" He put his hand on my shoulder and caressed it with his thumb. He leaned in and said, "You're really cute." I reached for my beer bottle and grabbed it by the neck, thumb pointing down.

My friend Norman knew me well enough to know what I was about to do. He quickly grabbed my hand, which was gripping my beer bottle by the neck, and held it. "Easy there, little sis," he said gently.

I looked at Norman. He stared back at me intensely. I felt like we were animals communicating telepathically. I looked up to the sexist who had his hand on my shoulder. The man looked from me to the beer bottle where my friend's hand was gripping mine. I was holding the bottle in the way you would hold it to grab it like a weapon and bash someone over the head with it.

The sexist let go of my shoulder, realizing what I'd almost done. "Umm, okay. Okay," he said and sidestepped away from me, taking things in.

He paid his tab and left, telling us briskly that he'd see us around. Norman let go of my hand. He gave me some advice. "You can't do that here. This isn't New York City. Everyone will hear about it. It's a small town. Everyone knows him. People like him. You'll have to see him again, walking down the street, probably tomorrow, and the next day, and the next. You won't be able to live here if you do things like that." And I knew he was right. I was too reactive.

There was something special about that moment for me. Norman didn't act like I was wrong to want to do what I almost did, or like I was crazy. He calmly explained to me what I had to *not do* to survive. In a few minutes, he'd reached in and took hold of the shock dial that this world had installed in my electrified heart, and turned it down from a ten to a five, where it rested, though readied, for several years.

And this is odd to say, but maybe I needed to have that moment with a *man* I loved and trusted. Maybe I needed to know a man could at least somewhat understand why I might feel so violent. I needed to connect with a male friend over this to at least feel somewhat calmer, not to be told I was insane or blowing things out of proportion, but that the way I was reacting to things most people viewed as mild sexism, at best, was understandable, but wasn't going to work out well for me in the long run.

And since we are on this subject, I would like to note that my friend Norman and I lived together as roommates for eight months, spent a lot of time together when I was in my twenties, even sometimes sharing a bed when we were traveling. And I know that in some moments of our friendship he found me attractive, but me, *all* of me, as a whole person, and he never sexually assaulted me, and he never sexually harassed me. I never once thought he might. And I am glad he stopped me from hitting that sexist over the head with a glass bottle.

*　*　*

I'm not saying everything I did then was great, but I also don't actually regret most things. I really didn't understand how young I was when I was twenty-two. But I *was* young, and while many women around me could take this stuff, I couldn't. I saw every sexist encounter horribly magnified.

I was listening to Karen Finley's spoken-word album *A Certain Level of Denial* every day, sometimes multiple times a day, like it was music, like it was my favorite rock album. This was a gritty spoken-word performance dealing with subjects of homophobia, violence, and rape. It wasn't music. It was more than a little disturbing, but I loved it. Sometimes I would even put it on during office hours at Tribes and all the interns had to listen to it.

I wouldn't have fucked with me then, and that's what Steve Cannon told everyone, "Don't fuck with her" (the "or she'll kick the shit out of you" was implied). I'm proud of this in some way, but it's also sad to me because until I was about fourteen, I was a pacifist. I believed earnestly in pacifism. I believed that even if someone used violence against you, it was wrong to use violence back. Because violence was wrong, in and of itself. I lived as a pacifist throughout most of my childhood, but it never worked. Still, there will always be a tender place in my heart for the sensitive, idealistic girl I was before I finally started hitting back.

44

When I was twenty-three, living in upstate New
York, I made friends with a man who was a few years
older than me. He developed a crush on me. I rejected his
advances. To be clear, I wasn't offended by this in any way.
He had a crush on me and he let me know that. He wasn't
some dude who just met me at a bar and wouldn't take no
for an answer. He was my friend, and he was attracted to me
and had romantic feelings for me, and I was not offended by
that in any way.

Like I said, I told him I wasn't interested in dating him.
He continued to act shy and nervous around me and sometimes flirtatious, which, again, is fine. I've had crushes on
people. I'm attracted to people. I know what it's like. And
I'm very capable of saying yes to sex and romance when I feel
it, too. I'm not offended by someone letting me know they
have a crush on me. I really enjoyed his company. I really
liked being friends with him. I thought he was weird and
interesting.

One night, we were together at a party for a club that
was breaking ground. The building was still under construction and a bunch of artists in the area were invited
to this performance party, thrown by the owners. I was
standing with this man and a group of five or six mutual

friends in the unfinished kitchen. We were all chatting after a performance.

This is hard to explain, because what he did was so weird. He'd been flirty with me that night and we were all jovially talking in a group. I don't remember exactly what I said, but it was funny and everyone laughed. Suddenly, he leapt forward and jumped on me.

I mean he fully tackled me.

He jumped on me, knocking me onto my back on the cement floor, and landed on top of me.

He'd tackled me to the ground and was on top of me. He started heavy petting and trying to kiss me (this all happened within a few seconds). Then I heard him screaming and felt him pulling away from me.

He stood up and was holding his hand to his neck. I sat up from where I was lying. "You fucking bit me!" he screamed. He held his hand out and looked at it, and I could see from where I was sitting that there was a small amount of blood on his fingers and neck.

I stood up and dusted myself off. "She fucking bit me!" he screamed at our group of friends. One of my male friends who was standing there yelled at him, "What the fuck are you doing? What the hell did you expect her to do?"

He looked me in the eyes. I had no thoughts in my head, no feelings at all. I didn't even realize I'd bitten him. I still don't remember biting him. But there was definitely a bite mark on his neck and I had broken the skin.

"You bit me," he said again. I stared at him blankly. "Seriously?" he chided me. For a brief moment I actually felt guilty. Then everyone started shouting things at him along the lines of, "What the fuck were you doing? That wasn't cool!" He turned and left the party.

Weirdly, I remained cordial with him after that. It was a small town and I saw him often in group settings. I didn't want to "cause drama." He didn't flirt with me anymore. He didn't try to date me, he didn't tell me had a crush on me, and he never assaulted me again.

We got along. But I really wish we could've gotten along without that incident.

* * *

I'd actually totally forgotten about this, but I was in upstate New York at Club Helsinki with my friend Joseph many years later, in 2017. He was performing a sold-out show there. We walked backstage and through the now-finished kitchen, and I turned to Joseph and said in a funny singsong voice, "Oh, hey! I was at a party here. I was sexually assaulted here."

"Oh how lovely. Here too?" Joseph said, and we laughed and laughed.

45

When I was twenty-four, I moved back to New York City, to Bushwick in Brooklyn. For several weeks, the man at the deli on my corner went from shaking my hand to *taking* my hand and kissing it whenever I bought something from him. I allowed this because, stupidly, I didn't want to be rude. He was an old man who shook my hand and sometimes kissed it in a joking manner, like this was a funny thing he was doing for my amusement. But I didn't like it. Though I "allowed it," it was mostly because when he grabbed my hand he was forceful. I would have had to cause a scene to pull it away.

One day, when I was picking up an egg sandwich, he took my hand, pulled me in toward him, grabbed me by the back of my head from across the counter, and attempted to forcibly tongue-kiss me.

I shoved and smacked him and then he bit my face so hard it left a mark. Yes. He *bit my face.* My right cheek. At the deli. In public. Okay.

46

When I was twenty-three, I was playing racquetball with my girlfriend on a gorgeous beach on Long Island. It was a late summer day, somewhat chilly, so we were both wearing sweatshirts and jeans on the beach. At one point, when we took a break from hitting the ball, we realized there were two men, who were totally unconnected to one another, sitting on opposite sides near us, masturbating.

It was a sure thing. They both had their dicks out, fully exposed, and were staring at us while jacking off. Two of them. One on our left. One on our right. And they didn't know each other. I just feel like I have to say that twice.

"Are you fucking kidding me?" my girlfriend shouted. I took the small ball we'd been playing racquetball with and threw it at one man's head. He ducked and smiled, then licked his lips at me. He did not stop masturbating.

My girlfriend (and I do mean lesbian partner) walked up to the other man, who was a white, well-dressed businessman type with a nice bag sitting next to him. She picked up his bag and walked it over to the ocean.

He stood, holding his crotch, his pants at his feet, and started waddling behind her, shouting "No, no, no!" She threw his bag into the ocean as he screamed.

"Fuck you!" she told him and then again, in Spanish. The

other man, who looked more like a not-well-off-at-all troll, got up and ran away as she headed over to him.

When we lamented the story to a heterosexual couple on the beach later, the man of the couple told us we shouldn't come to the beach "alone together." Two women . . . "alone" . . . "together."

Alone. Together.

47

I was twenty-three, walking down the sidewalk to the grocery store. A man came up to me and my girlfriend on an empty street in the middle of the afternoon and asked how long we'd lived in the neighborhood. We'd moved there a week before. He was standing slightly behind a street divider. I'd seen him around the neighborhood often.

As I began what I thought was a pleasant conversation with a new neighbor, my girlfriend grabbed my arm and tugged me away. When I moved, I saw around to the other side of the divider. He had his hand in his pants, obviously had an erection, and seemed to be beginning to jack off while he talked to me.

48

When I was twenty-three, I was walking through Tompkins Square Park at dusk (a typical route from work and usually well-trafficked). A man standing by a tree ran up to me, shouted "Come here," and tried to grab me by my waist (like grab my whole body) to abduct me.

I jumped and barely got out of reach of his grasp, then we both took off at a dead run. He chased me to the edge of the park where I ran toward a group of people walking a dog. I shouted at them for help. He stopped, turned, and ran away. One of the people called the police, but the man was long gone. The police came. They told me I shouldn't walk alone at night, which is, of course, impossible.

49

When I was twenty-five, I was a grant writer for a
social-justice nonprofit. I had my own office on a floor that
was shared with another social-justice nonprofit. At least twice
a week, a man in his fifties who worked for the other nonprofit
on the floor would knock on my door, step into my office and
close the door behind himself, so that we were the only ones in
the room, and tell me a dirty joke. This typically ended with a
reference to his penis, him motioning to his crotch, humping
the air, pantomiming jacking off, and so on.

I would stare at him, annoyance showing on my face,
and say dryly, "Okay," hoping he would take a hint. I began
negotiating his physical position in an unspoken way. When
he would knock on my door, I would roll the chair back
from my desk, blocking the doorway, so that he couldn't
enter, and he was forced to stand in the hall (instead of inside
my office with the door closed) and tell me the dirty joke,
which he did, and continued doing, regardless of my forcing
him into the hallway, for nearly two months.

I didn't know what else to do. I was one of the younger
employees and had just begun working there. He seemed to
know everyone.

Finally, another woman, who was somewhat my supe-
rior and about four years older than me, was working

in my office one day (which she did twice a month) and the man came to the doorway, and told me a sexual joke: "An Irish guy walks into a bar with a ship wheel hanging off of his penis. The bartender says, 'Why is there a ship wheel hanging on your dick?'" This joke ended with him motioning to his crotch, which was near my face, and thrusting at me. "'I don't know, but it's driving me nuts!'" I stared blankly at him. He smiled and said, "Well, have a good day," and left.

My coworker turned to me and asked, "What the hell was that?" I told her he did that all the time. She said, "No, no."

She stood and motioned for me to follow her. We went into the president's office and she told him what the man was doing. Our boss said he would speak to this man's boss about it. The next day, I was standing in the hallway with her and the president and the man walked past, tapped me on the shoulder, interrupting my conversation with my bosses, and told me an awkward, sexist dirty joke right in front of them. He then squeezed my shoulder, smiled, told me to have a great day and continued down the hall. The president looked to my female coworker, totally dumbfounded. It was pretty gutsy for the man to have done this in front of him.

"That's what I was talking about," she said. The president's jaw was hanging open. He told me that would never happen again and it immediately stopped.

This woman, my coworker who stood up for me, didn't particularly like me. She didn't hate me. But I think she found me annoying.

She was serious, smart, and deliberate. She was a Catholic, black activist who was getting her master's degree. She had been with the organization for many years and acted much older than her age and definitely older than me. I was young and overly talkative, queer, punk, generally weirdly dressed, and we had bumped heads in conversations about Christianity and liberal versus leftist politics. I thought she was cool and sometimes babbled at her too much to try to impress her, and I think in conversations about racial activism she found some of my ideas naïve, "young, not fully formed, leftist white girl" notions. I mean, I knew I annoyed her no matter how much I wanted her to think I was as cool as I thought she was.

And I always hear men talk about how much women hate each other. And even though she may have sometimes been rolling her eyes or even complaining about me behind my back, she knew I did good work. She valued me as a person and a worker, she cared about my well-being, and she immediately took steps to ensure I would not be sexually harassed at work by this man, without a second thought. She protected me when I wasn't able to protect myself. Because the truth is that, ultimately, women look out for one another.

50

I was twenty-five and excited to be working directly under one of the top organization officials at a nonprofit I'd always respected. It was a mid-level position, but the job description involved working directly under a man I admired a lot professionally and politically. Throughout the first couple of months, I became aware that he never called me into meetings, rarely spoke to me, and when I spoke to him, he tried to keep the conversations as short as possible.

I had a lot of ideas I wanted to share with him. I wanted to impress him. I wanted him to be aware of me and I also wanted a chance to learn from him professionally.

I was trying to figure out what I'd done wrong. When I lamented to a coworker that I thought this man must not like me or respect me, my coworker informed me that this man had carried on an affair (he was married) with a young woman who was my age, who occupied my position previously. It had been a bit of a scandal, so everyone else knew why he was keeping a "safe distance" from me.

This affair had been consensual, although questionably appropriate given the power dynamics implied by the disparate authority of their positions. But why did I have to pay the price for that, professionally and intellectually? Just because I was also a woman, there was something inherently "dangerous" about me? I, a completely unwitting and unrelated person, had to bear the burden of his guilt?

Yes. This is something we learn to navigate. As women, we are constantly guilty. It is a knowledge I've had since I was young. It is always there under the surface, even when I'm unaware of it. I remember a poem by Adrienne Rich in which she said something along the lines of, "When I was pregnant, that was the only time, in public, as a woman, I didn't feel guilty of something."

Of course, I was recently talking to a woman who was pregnant as a teenager and she recounted how difficult that experience was, primarily because of the way people treated her in public. When she was pregnant, she wasn't only guilty. She was condemned. She'd already failed. And the fault of this failure was hers alone. And oddly, the people who made her feel the guiltiest about having a baby were also anti-choice. So, how can we win? We can't win.

In this system of thinking, we lose wherever we turn. If we don't have sex, we are guilty of "really wanting it." If we do, we are guilty of giving in and of temptation. I was hired to a job where I had done absolutely nothing sexual with anyone and I was implicitly guilty of what I may have eventually incited. Guilty because I was a similar age as a woman who had "incited" inappropriate sexual relations before me. And of course, she was the guilty one there too. She had been fired. The man in charge of the organization had stayed.

As soon as I came into this position, I was a reminder of the previous indiscretions of a man in power, who I'd never interacted with and somehow, I felt the stigma of that guilt inside myself as well, transferred to me by others who unconsciously agreed I was guilty. Amazing.

51

When I was twenty-five, my girlfriend and I traveled to Venezuela for two weeks to attend a radical literary conference in Caracas. I was working for a small press and my purpose there was to collect poetry from Venezuelan poets as part of a larger anthology the press was publishing, Poetry from the Axis of Evil.

This was a response to the Bush regime and the lack of information allowed in from certain countries at the time. I was a guest of the last Venezuelan cultural attaché assigned to the United States and had met with them in New York. In Caracas, I was officially a guest of the government at the time and was staying with the attaché's mother. I was given different "hosts" on different days—people in the government and publishing world who were to take me around to different literary events each day and introduce me to authors. I say all this to drive home the fact that I was there in a professional capacity and the people who met me, for the most part, treated me respectfully, knowing all of this.

One day, my girlfriend and I were "hosted" by the secretary of culture. He seemed to be one rung below the minister of culture of Venezuela. He was an older man, in his late fifties, a poet, and was also a head editor for the Venezuelan government poetry press. My partner and I were not always out with everyone as a lesbian couple on this trip. She was Spanish and often acted as my translator for more complex conversations, though, most people also spoke English to me (one of many privileges I had as an American).

After spending the entire day with this secretary of culture, and after he had spent the day telling me about his own feminist poetry, leftist and communist revolutionary ideals, and his theories of radical publishing, he took me and my girlfriend to hear a reading by the minister of culture.

I sat, my girlfriend on my right, the secretary of culture on my left, in a large, old, dark theater, listening to the minister sing and read poetry accompanied by a guitar player.

After a few minutes, I felt the hand of the secretary grasp my left hand and begin caressing it. He leaned in and began whispering in my ear, his breath on my neck: "You are so damn sexy." He said, "How old are you?" He caressed my hand. "You couldn't be a day over seven. You are a peculiar girl, no? How old are you? Seven. Oh, you couldn't be a day over seven, little girl."

52

I was in my mid-twenties. I met my friend Danny for a beer at a bar in the East Village before attending an art opening. It was late afternoon. The bar was mostly empty, except for two white men who were sitting a couple stools down from us. One of the men "took a shine" to me. He struck up a conversation with me, interrupting my conversation with my good friend, about how physically attractive he found me.

He came around the bar, put his arm around me, and squeezed my shoulders. He asked to buy me a drink. He asked for my phone number. He tried to give me his. All of this I clearly, repeatedly, and at points, angrily rejected. His male friend kept pulling him away, trying to talk to him and get him to leave me alone. My friend Danny even told him to cut it out. But he kept yelling across the bar. Danny and I finished our drinks quickly and paid to leave, after only being there about thirty minutes, even though we had more than an hour to kill.

As we left the bar, the man followed me out onto the sidewalk, still telling me that he wanted to take me out for dinner and holding out a card with his number on it. I was wearing a skirt and when we were standing outside in the daylight he noticed my legs, which I've rarely shaved since I was seventeen.

"Oh my God," he said, almost yelling. "Why don't you shave your legs? That's disgusting. You're so beautiful. But you gotta shave your legs." He held his card out to me. "I mean, I'll still take you out on a nice date and everything, but you gotta shave your legs, okay?"

Danny and I burst out laughing. It was too much. "I'm not going on a fucking date with you!" I squealed, still laughing. "And I'm not shaving my fucking legs!"

I flipped him off and Danny and I walked away, but he was still yelling from behind me, "You're hot, but you gotta shave your legs."

I had shown zero interest in this man, repeatedly rejected him, all but begged him to leave me alone, and he still felt emboldened enough to tell me what I should do with my body to please him. He still thought his opinion of my body mattered.

53

When I was in my mid-twenties, a woman I was close to was brutally attacked by a stranger in an attempted rape, which was also probably an attempted murder.

I was with her moments after it happened. I'd never seen anyone endure this level of violence in real life, before or since. The scene was bloody and horrific. I'll never get it out of my mind. She looked like what I imagined an injured soldier would look like after a gruesome battle. But she was just a small woman, walking alone at night.

Witnessing this level of violence enacted upon a woman I cared for changed me for the rest of my life. The toxic aftermath of this trauma also destroyed our relationship.

This attack occurred just a couple of years after two of my lovers and one of my best friends were all violently raped in the Midwest. That was one of the reasons I'd moved away. And now there was this horror in New York City. Within two years, a fourth person I was close to had been violently, sexually attacked.

This incident spawned a stint of magical thinking for me that lasted several years. I began to believe that there was something spiritually wrong with me—perhaps supernatural, like a curse—that was causing women I loved to be raped. Every time it happened it got closer to me and more gruesome. I became paranoid, controlling, and overprotective of my partners when they were interacting with heterosexual men. I no longer trusted straight men. I feared that every woman I was with would be raped and that somehow it would be my fault. It was obviously an illogical belief, but it was stuck like a pin in my brain. It made me a bad girlfriend at times.

Beyond this magical thinking, the logical part of me understood that so many women I was close to were raped in such a short amount of time because violence against women is an epidemic. I felt like there was an actual, physical war happening and only women were aware we were fighting it.

The man who attacked my friend didn't want her money. He didn't want her things. He wanted access to *her* and was willing to kill her for it. And that is a knowledge women carry with us when we're walking down the street alone. This could happen to any of us and has happened to too many of us. I personally know multiple women who have experienced this type of violent attack.

There is little way to describe how deeply I detest the fact that so many women I've loved and couldn't protect have been emotionally and physically maimed by the same bigotry, over and over.

54

I was twenty-six and managing an art project with my then-girlfriend, who is a visual artist. We had done a large collaborative public art project that involved an image she'd painted, including some of my text and hers, being printed out and mounted on a large, high-standing billboard in Brooklyn.

We rented out a space on an aesthetically gorgeous building on the Crown Heights/Bed-Stuy border that had this giant metal, permanent billboard frame on its roof, overlooking the street. The billboard had remained empty for years.

As the project manager, I raised most of the money to cover the $10,000 project budget successfully (my girlfriend raised the rest). I also dealt with the ad company that rented out the actual billboard space. I oversaw the terms of the contract and paid for the billboard space, printing, and mounting. When the billboard went up, they used the wrong material and it immediately was torn out by the wind, which is quite forceful six stories high.

This was a $5,000 rental. That's what my partner and I paid for this job and it was botched. I went in the first day I could and spoke to the manager of the billboard company.

He was religious and wouldn't even shake my hand when

I held it out, which is awkward when you're coming in to discuss business. It immediately placed me in the position of being a girl, something very different than him, feeling guilty about making him possibly desire me.

I explained to the man that I wanted the billboard replaced with the tight mesh material I'd ordered. (They hadn't used the material I'd originally requested.) The material I wanted was small mesh and you can't actually see that it is mesh from far away. You can only tell it's mesh if you're standing close to it. He argued with me and told me that the vinyl would work better because mesh would be see-through. But I knew this wasn't the case at the height this billboard stood. And, of course, the vinyl *hadn't* worked. It had torn and blown down immediately. Finally, he insisted that I had actually originally ordered the vinyl, but I had a copy of the contract on me and it clearly stated I'd ordered the mesh. I took it out and showed it to him.

When he saw the contract, he became angry. He waved his hands at me and said, "Hey, why don't you just calm down?" He pointed to a chair. "You sit down and be quiet. Okay? Just sit down and wait here, young lady." I stared at the chair. He left the room.

We had already gone round and round for nearly an hour. He was being nothing but rude and dismissive, even though I am the one who had signed him a check for $5,000 the week before and handed it to him. And it went through. I'd paid for this project, as far as he knew, with my own money. But he had zero respect for me. I had researched billboards. I knew exactly what I wanted. I knew what would work on a structure as high up as the one he owned.

I went outside instead of waiting in the chair and called my friend Danny. He's a teacher and poet. He's a well-spoken heterosexual man. I knew that was what I needed. I needed a man to speak for me.

Danny knew absolutely nothing about the project I was

doing. Nothing whatsoever. I had not mentioned it to him in any way previously. He knew nothing about billboards. He knew nothing about the location of the piece. He knew nothing about anything that I was doing that day. I called him and asked him for this favor. He thought it was funny, but he understood and agreed. I told him to write down what I needed him to say, word for word. It was the exact same thing I had been repeating over and over for an hour to the man without any results. I told him I was going to go upstairs and tell the man that he, Danny, was my boss and that he was pissed. Then I was going to give the man the phone. I said that Danny should talk to him however he would talk to a man to get them to do something, but make sure to say exactly, word for word, what I had said about the billboard material.

I went back upstairs. The business owner was standing in the lobby and as soon as he saw me, he tore into me, doubling down, "I thought you left! I told you to sit here and wait. There's no way we are going to reprint this entire poster on mesh. Mesh will look strange. We're putting the vinyl back up, blah blah blah . . ." I interrupted him and told him that my boss, the project manager, was on the phone.

This, of course, was a lie. *I* was the project manager. I was my own boss. I said, "He really wants to talk to you." The man took the phone and actually went into the other room with my phone and closed the door.

He came out four minutes later, tops. He handed me the phone. "Okay," he said. "Okay. We got it. We figured it all out."

"What did you decide?" I asked.

He told me, "No worries. Talk to your boss. He'll tell you. We got it all figured out."

I said that I needed *him* to tell me. But he was getting mad again and refused. He said, "This is between me and your boss, okay? It's all worked out. Talk to your boss. He'll let you know."

I sighed and said, "Fine," and left, no handshake. No explanation. I was so pissed.

I called Danny back. Danny couldn't believe the man wouldn't even tell me what they decided. But he said he'd agreed to reprint the billboard on the material that I had actually ordered. "Are you sure?" I asked. "He was totally against that. What did you say?"

Danny said, "I didn't say anything except exactly what I wrote down when we were talking. I said, 'Look I really need this done this week. I need . . .'" and then he repeated the words he'd written down that I'd dictated to him. And the man had simply responded, "Okay, okay, you got it. We'll fix it. It'll be done Monday night."

And a few days later, it was fixed. They reprinted the billboard on the correct material, and it was properly installed. It looked beautiful. And it didn't rip or get blown down again. It stayed up for months.

This makes me fucking crazy. How many times have I said something and then a man has turned around and said the exact same thing I said, only to have the men in the room respond positively, after they'd ignored me or shot me down? I cannot count how many times this has happened. But this is maybe the most blatant example of that, since the man repeating my words was doing so consciously, at my behest, literally reading the script I gave him.

55

This one is the fact that from 2007 to 2014, every transgender woman I was close to (and there were a few) who came out/transitioned to living as a woman lost her job within a year of doing so. Most of them had to move out of New York City because of this.

56

I was twenty-seven and was walking home alone at night from a party. It was about 11 o'clock. I weighed about 115 pounds. I was wearing a revealing leather dress. The street I was walking on was mostly empty and, at some point, I noticed a large group of children walking behind me. They were all boys between the ages of twelve and fourteen. There were about eight of them.

They were carrying baseball bats and sticks. One had the pole of a broom without the broom on it. One of them had a hockey stick. One of them had a dog on a leash. They walked up closer to me from behind and started tapping their sticks on the ground. Then suddenly, they were around me, circling me, tapping their sticks on the ground faster. I picked up my pace. They picked up theirs and then, one of the boys swung a bat at my head. I ducked and took off at a dead run and all of the boys started chasing me.

I was certain at that moment, and there was absolutely no question in me, they wanted to kill me and would if I didn't get away. They wanted to beat me to death. I ran for two blocks with them chasing close behind me swinging things and shouting. I was so terrified that I immediately ran into the first open place I saw. It was a deli, and I ran straight through, knocking things over and shoving people out of the way.

I saw a door in the back of the deli that no doubt led to a storage closet. I ran right for it, grabbed the knob, and started tugging at the door, wanting to lock myself in. But it was already locked and I couldn't open it, and then I literally started clawing at the door and screaming at the top of my lungs.

Everyone in the deli was staring at me. I turned and watched the doorway, expecting the boys to come barreling through. All of a sudden a large man wearing a novelty T-shirt that read (I kid you not) CALL DA POLICE came through the door screaming, "What the fuck what the fuck what the fuck!"

He ran toward me, yelling, "Are you okay? What the fuck?" He grabbed me by the shoulders and hugged me. Some of the people were looking at him with concern. He was a large, black man, well over six feet tall. He was a huge guy, quite muscular, and I think people were thinking it was him I'd been running from. But I grabbed on to him instinctively and hugged him back, holding on tight.

I was so glad he was there and had no idea who he was.

He took me by the shoulders, looked at me and said, "Man, those kids were trying to kill you." Then he turned to everyone in the deli and said, "They were trying to *kill* her. Man! I saw what they were doing to you." He was all revved up. "That was fucked up!" He told the deli guy, "These kids were chasing her. They were trying to kill her."

Everyone in the deli came over and the man who owned it grabbed many different juices out of the fridge, handed them to me with a bag of chips, and told me to drink and eat. I didn't want to eat or drink right then, but he made me take at least a sip of orange juice, which was cute enough for me to find it humorous even in that moment.

The large man with the CALL DA POLICE shirt told me

that he had been driving down the street in his car and saw what was happening. He had pulled over outside the deli and chased the kids away. He said they were all gone. But I stayed there, called a cab, and got a ride the rest of the way home.

I moved to a different neighborhood two months later.

57

It was the night of the Obama election. I was overjoyed that he'd won. I was with my partner and a couple of friends, and we moved from dancing in the streets (people were actually dancing on top of buses) to a nightclub that was showing his acceptance speech on a big screen. The room was crowded.

My girlfriend left to go to the bathroom and a man started hitting on me. I told him, annoyed, that I was there with my girlfriend, that I was a dyke, and that I just wanted to watch the acceptance speech. He was a well-dressed white kid in his mid-twenties. He was much, much taller than me and skinny. He told me I should try a man sometime. I told him to fuck off. He told me he wanted to buy me a drink. I angrily responded that I had already told him no. "Leave me the fuck alone," I said forcefully.

I turned away from him as best I could, but it was almost shoulder to shoulder in there. He reached forward and lifted my hat off my head. I turned and stared at him. He patted me on the top of the head like I was a child and gave me a shit-eating grin. "You're adorable!" he said, loudly, slowly, smiling down patronizingly at me. Then he put my hat back down on my head and nodded, chuckling.

"If you touch me again," I said calmly, "your balls are going to be coming out of your nose."

He managed to scoot through the packed crowd and get far away from me.

58

When I was twenty-seven, I realized I was forgetting many things that happened, and I felt like I was losing my mind because of the constant sexual harassment I was experiencing. As a mindfulness technique, I decided to keep a daily log.

The following posts are from a sexual harassment log I kept in my journal for only one week, when I was twenty-seven years old. To really make it apparent how much I'm forgetting and omitting from this already long list, this is what it looked like if I logged it daily. Throughout my twenties, street harassment was a constant aspect of my existence as a woman living in a city.

July 16, 2010: Sat in the park on the grass with my lover. Man came up and sat behind me and pulled his penis out and began masturbating. We responded by yelling at him and leaving.

July 16, 2010: Two hours later, at a different place in the park, a man with a light strapped to his head approached me and my girlfriend, saying he was going to sit with us in the secluded area we'd retreated to, near the street. I told him to leave us alone. He said he was a cop. He was definitely not a cop.

As he continued toward us, I approached him, trying to

be protective of my girlfriend and attempted to kick him in the balls, which is harder than it seems. He kept jumping away from me, holding his hands out, then repeatedly tried to grab me by the ankle. We finally started shouting, hoping to draw the attention of people on a nearby sidewalk, and walked/jogged away quickly, cutting our Central Park date short.

July 16 2010: When I was going into my apartment in the early evening, a man jogged over, stood in front of me, blocked my door, and asked me, "Are you looking to get pregnant tonight?"

I told him, "No, I'm looking to walk down the street with some amount of dignity. Do you have a problem with that?"

The man responded with, "Obama is president!" (He was black.)

I lost it on him. I was actually coming home early because I'd been jacked off on earlier that day and harassed by another man after that, and now I couldn't even get into my home, where I was retreating to try and feel safe for the night.

I started screaming, ranting at him about rape and harassment, telling him to go fuck himself, and I think I even nonsensically referenced waiting for the day *Michelle* Obama became president.

The man responded, "I wasn't trying to start a rap-off. I was giving you a *compliment*." His friends stood nearby laughing at us. He stepped away and allowed me to enter my building.

July 17, 2010: Man followed me around the Goodwill licking his lips at me. I finally turned to him and yelled, "*What do you want?*" He did not respond but gave me one last gross lip-licking, looked me up and down, and then left.

July 18, 2010: I sat with a friend at a table outside a café eating a salad. An older Russian man with a cane walked by and stopped in front of my table. He turned to face me, pointed at me then to himself, and in broken English said, "You like to me. I like to you." I did not respond in any way. He repeated himself once, louder, and pointed to me and himself again, in case I did not understand. "You like me? I like you." I still did not respond. Then he sneered meanly and said, "Smells like *fish*," spit on the ground in front of me and left.

July 19, 2010: Walking down the street. Young man clicks his tongue at me like I am a small animal, says in a sexual voice, "Come here, cutie!" Holds his hand out as I pass in front of him repeating, "Come here, come here, come here, sexy," in high-pitched tones . . . like I am a small animal. I do not respond. "Bitch!" I hear him yell at my back.

July 22, 2010: I'd experienced so much aggressive harassment over the past few days in my neighborhood that I decided to take a summer scarf and drape it around my shoulders to cover the bare skin I was revealing by wearing a tank top.

It was hot and I wanted to wear a tank top, but did not think I would make it from my house to the subway, then to work, without this intense harassment that was making me crazy. As I exited my apartment and attempted to walk down my stairs, I encountered a maintenance man who was also making his way down the stairs in front of me. He saw me, turned to me, smiled, and said hello. I smiled back and said hello. He then proceeded to walk down three flights of stairs backwards, facing me, looking me up and down the whole time and smiling at me, like we were doing something together.

My skin crawled. I couldn't even say hello to this man without him taking it as some sort of romantic or sexual invitation.

As soon as I reached the bottom of the stairs I took the scarf that was around my shoulders and wrapped it around my head, instinctually. I walked past him quickly with the scarf fully covering my hair, my shoulders, and part of my face.

I made my way from my apartment to the subway in relative peace that day, with the exception of one young construction worker who actually stepped into my path as I was walking, to make eye contact with me around the scarf, and repeated "Hello, hello, mami."

59

When I was twenty-seven, my girlfriend and I went to Atlantic City with a straight white male friend of mine in his mid-forties. We had fun all day and part of the evening, going around and playing the slots and tables and seeing the sights. When we were with my male friend everything was fine. No one bothered us. Later, my girlfriend and I decided to go out on our own to spend a few hours together, romantically, on the boardwalk.

We were only out for about thirty minutes though, because we were so intensely sexually harassed by so many men, with the final straw being a man who followed us for several yards catcalling us at close range. We ignored him and kept walking and he finally grabbed my arm and said into my ear, "I'm gonna fuck you, bitch. But I'm not *just* going to fuck you. I'm going to make you call 911! You're gonna have to call 911!" We ran away from him and went back to the hotel.

I was twenty-seven and was walking down the street holding hands with my girlfriend. An extremely large man (over six feet tall, sturdily built) punched my girlfriend in the stomach hard as he walked by, without missing a step. Then turned the corner, disappearing into the NYC foot traffic.

61

I was twenty-seven and I had just broken up with my partner of three years. I spent the night at a lesbian bar in the West Village, attempting to drown my sorrows, but I didn't have a good time. I'd had two drinks and was still grieving. The drinks hadn't helped. I was in a horrible mood. It was cold outside. I was walking from the bar to the subway, and a large man started following me.

As I walked by him, he turned, started walking with me and said, "Hey, your husband's a lucky man." I didn't respond, so he said again, closer to me and louder, "Your husband is a *lucky* man." I still didn't respond, he kept walking with me, and he reached out and took hold of my elbow. "Excuse me," he said, pulling at my arm, "I said, your husband . . ."

I turned and started punching him, screaming, "I don't have a fucking husband!" He was at least six feet tall, more than twice my size, and I was hitting him in his arm without even thinking about the consequences of this if he decided to retaliate. He took a step back and told me, "If you keep hitting me, I'm gonna fuck you up."

I grabbed him by the collar of his coat, putting as much of my weight on it as I could, lifting myself by his collar, and pulled him down so that he was bending over, and then

I screamed in his face, "Do you think you can fuck me up worse than I already am?"

He put his hands in the air and took two steps back. I let go of him. He told me he was going to call the police. I told him to do it and kept walking at a brisk pace. A few blocks later, I turned and looked back, and I saw police lights on the corner right where I'd been. He actually called the police. I felt so crazed—I'd scared this large man who was harassing me enough that *he* called 911. I laughed and got on the subway.

62

When I was twenty-seven, I was at a supposedly queer dance party in Berlin, Germany. I was dancing with a girl who had been flirting with me all night. A young man came up behind me, grabbed my waist and pulled me into him quickly, slid his hands up under my shirt, and fondled my breasts with his hands against my bare skin. I pulled away from him, but he wouldn't let me go. The girl started yelling at him. I finally got loose from him and shoved him.

The girl and I left the dance floor, spent many hours together, and had a nice time. Then, when I was leaving the party, as I walked to the exit, a different man who was standing by the door reached out and grabbed my breasts.

63

When I was twenty-seven, I was visiting Paris.
It was right after sunset, and I was sitting on a bench near
the Eiffel Tower. I had moved a bit away from the crowd of
tourists to write in my journal. After I finished writing, I
decided to cut through a small slice of the park to get back to
the road. A minute after I began walking through the park, I
noticed a tall man close behind me.

He was over six feet tall, lanky, but muscular. I turned to
look at him because he was so close. He smiled down at me,
hovering about a foot away. He had a horrible look in his
eyes. He said, "Hello, lover" in a French accent and lunged
forward, grabbing for me with both hands.

I somehow avoided his grasp and we both took off at a
dead run. This was the fourth time, I realized, that I was
running for my life from a strange man in public.

That chase seemed to last forever. I made it to the sidewalk and found a group of three men walking. I literally ran
into them and grabbed one by the arm. I was screaming and
crying.

The men saw the man chasing me. They turned and stared
at him. He stopped, turned, and ran away, disappearing back
into the darkening park. The men comforted me in broken
English as I tried to relate to them what happened. They

walked me to a place where I could get a cab and told me I shouldn't walk alone at night, which, as I've noted before, is impossible.

64

When I was twenty-eight, I was walking with a
female friend, smoking a cigarette and talking to her. A
group of three well-dressed white men who looked to be in
their late forties were standing next to a warehouse, talking.

As we approached them, one of the men noticed me.
As I got close, he suddenly stepped out into the sidewalk,
blocking my path, and crouched like a football player preparing to intercept a runner, with his arms spread wide, and
said, "Come here, sweetie."

He grabbed at me, but stopped with his hands and body
about an inch from mine, as I held my lit cigarette right
up to his eye, the hot cherry a few inches from his eyeball,
threatening him. "Fucking try it," I told him.

He looked shocked and stepped aside. I kept walking and
took up the conversation again with my female friend. Once
we were away from the men, she turned and grabbed my
shoulders. "What the hell was that? Can we acknowledge
what just happened for a minute?"

I realized I was so used to it, I didn't even break step when
a stranger on the street tried to grab me and what . . . literally
pick me up? Take me? God only knows what he was thinking
of doing.

65

I was twenty-eight and on the subway late at night. There were few other people on the subway, a handful of teenagers, one middle-aged couple, a pregnant woman sitting next to me, and a single middle-aged man who got up and began walking up and down the subway talking about men's and women's roles in society.

I was dressed butch, wearing dress shorts and a collared shirt, vest, and tie. I do not shave my legs. The man pointed to the pregnant woman and told everyone on the subway, "See, this is what a woman is supposed to look like! Be fruitful and multiply. How beautiful." Then he looked at me. He walked over to me and held the bar above where I was sitting, completely leaning over me, and said, "And what the fuck are you? I can't even tell if you're a man or a woman. This is unnatural. Look at this ugly bitch." He glanced around the car. Everyone was watching this. He leaned down close to my face, and inspected me. Then he said, "Oh, I know. You're a dyke." He started clapping his hands and laughing, shouting, "Dyke, dyke, dyke." The other people in the subway laughed (except the pregnant woman). I couldn't tell if this was nervous laughter or if they all actually hated me. Maybe both?

66

When I was twenty-eight, I tried to have a nice day at the Cloisters with my girlfriend, but we had to leave because within an hour, we were flashed by one man, followed by two others making sexual and antigay comments at us, and were also more mildly catcalled repeatedly by several other men. Taking a walk in the supposedly magnificent park was so unpleasant that we left. I've never gone back.

67

When I was twenty-eight, the man who worked at the only wine store in my neighborhood, where I often bought wine, verbally harassed me, asking me if I wanted him to "pop my cork," making kissing and sucking noises at me and licking his lips. At first, I ignored him (many deli men also do this if I'm alone). But he was so over the top, I told him point-blank to stop it the third time he did it. After that, he got more aggressive, so I quit going there altogether.

68

I was twenty-eight and got a new roommate through a reference from a female friend and former coworker. He was a straight, white male two years younger than me. I interviewed him and he seemed nice. He had a degree in philosophy and was also a writer. He had a good income (was from a fairly wealthy family in Long Island) and seemed like he'd be good for paying the rent on time. He was clean, well-spoken, queer-friendly (at least, he seemed so at first), and even shared my tastes in literature. I was happy to have found a good match.

About a week after he moved in, he stopped wearing clothes.

We lived in a small two-bedroom railroad, just me and him. He only wore his "tighty whities" when he was in the house. It was awkward. I am actually pretty comfortable with public nudity, but this nudity quickly began to feel directed at me.

I would go into my bedroom when he was hanging out in the kitchen in nothing but his thin underwear. He would often try to keep me there, talking nonstop about his personal life. I would find a way to remove myself and he often would then knock on my door and come into my room to chat with different excuses, such as not knowing how the shower worked or how to connect to the Internet. Once, he came into my room to ask about the Internet and sat on the edge of my bed in his undies and fidgeted with the modem (he said the connection was weak). While he was on the edge of my bed, he asked if I'd heard the neighbors having sex the night before. "Do you ever kinda like overhearing people having sex?" he asked.

I told him I didn't really think about it that much, unless it was something crazy.

He was intrigued. "What do you mean by crazy?"

"Oh, nothing." I didn't want to talk about this with him.

His behavior escalated a little every week. He started asking me for hugs when he was in his underwear. His Canadian girlfriend was mad at him, and when I would go into the kitchen to make food or wash the dishes, he would come out of his room, tell me about how mean she was, and ask me for hugs. One time, I patted his shoulder and he pulled me into a bear-hug embrace. The second time, I told him I'd been sick, and didn't want to get him sick too. The third time he did this, I told him, "I'm not a huggy person. So, I won't ever really want that." After this, he went into the bathroom and cried loudly enough that I could hear him from the kitchen.

I was in a nonmonogamous relationship at this point, so, because he was my roommate, he was able to glean some idea of my sex life. He'd met my girlfriend. She sometimes spent the night with me. Once, just a few days after my girlfriend had stayed over, I had a casual encounter with another woman. We'd come in during the late evening when I thought he was asleep. In the morning, I made my casual date some coffee and he walked through the kitchen in his underwear while she was sitting at the kitchen table. He said a brief hello, then he went back to his room. I rolled my eyes and apologized to my one-night date. She left as soon as her coffee was done, and he came back out to chat with me.

"Wow," he exclaimed. "How old was she? Cause she looked like she was eighteen!"

I stared at him blankly. "She's twenty-eight. She's an architect," I told him.

"Oh, really? Because she looked like she wasn't a day over eighteen!" I stood, walked past him, trying to ignore him, and washed our cups in the sink. He continued (still only in his underwear). "Well, it sounded like she had a good time."

"What?"

"Last night," he clarified, "It sounded like she had a good time."

I gave him a look that said, "what the fuck?" His bedroom was on the opposite side of the building from mine. Between his room and mine was a narrow hallway, a bathroom, an open kitchen, then a common space with a small table. I didn't think he could have heard anything from my room if he was in his. Had he been sitting at the kitchen table near my room all night, listening in while I had sex? I hated this thought. This was too much. I wanted to scream at him and tell him he had to move out right then and there, but I also didn't want to make a man I didn't know well, and with whom I was living, too angry.

"That's a weird thing to say." I told him, "I don't like this conversation. And also," I snapped, "why don't you ever wear pants? I have guests over sometimes and honestly, even for me, it's weird. It makes me uncomfortable."

He laughed this off. "Oh yeah. A lot of people have said that, 'why don't you put on some pants?' Ha! I don't like wearing clothes. Well, I have to get ready for work. See ya."

A couple weeks later, I started up a brief sexual liaison with a female friend of mine. We were having a great time, coming home from a fun dyke party and being flirty. I'd warned her about my roommate from hell, who, in addition to not wearing clothes, also was concerned about the amount of electricity we used. On top of this, he had peculiar eating habits. He'd boil an entire chicken, leave it in a pot in the fridge, and eat from it for a week. That was what he lived on, one full boiled chicken each week.

My friend and I came into the apartment in the evening, laughing and talking, only to find a steam-filled apartment, totally dark (to spare electricity), save for the eerie blue light above the stove, which he had turned on. He was standing in the near-darkness in his underwear, boiling a chicken. The whole apartment smelled of boiling chicken. He turned from where he stood, holding a wet wooden spoon in the air, in his underwear. "Hi," he said, "Did you have fun at your lesbo party?"

My friend and I laughed, squealed, and ran into my room. "Oh, yeah, we did." I shouted at him, shutting the door behind me. My friend named what he was doing "other-worldly kitchen scenes." She spent the night and left the next day, and, yes, we'd had sex. He also saw her leaving in the morning.

Two days later, my girlfriend came over. This was all too much for him. He'd just gotten a kitten. My girlfriend and I were dressed to go out to a formal event and he stopped me as we were walking through the kitchen to leave. He was glaring at me (and this time, he was fully dressed because I think he was planning on going out too). He picked up his kitten and started petting it. "Do you know if there's any special food I should feed a kitten this age?" he asked me. (I also had a cat.)

I did know. I told him he should feed it a higher-protein kitten food.

He gave me a weird look. He seemed agitated with me. "Yeah, I thought I should ask you. I thought you would know. You seem to know a hell of a lot more about pussies than I do, that's for goddamn sure."

I didn't even know what to say. My girlfriend rolled her eyes. I left awkwardly.

I wanted to ask him to move out. I felt like I was being regularly harassed in my own home, but I also constantly second-guessed myself. I wanted the problem to resolve itself somehow, because forcing a roommate to move out in New York City can turn into a long and difficult process.

I didn't see him for a few days. Then one morning, I was sitting at the kitchen eating my breakfast and he came out of his room into the kitchen in his thin, white underwear and he had an erection. He walked up to the table and started trying to talk to me, but I said, "You've got to be fucking kidding me," and stood and went into my room and slammed and locked the door.

I sent him an email later that day, after he'd gone to work, telling him I needed to have a conversation with him and I needed him to be fully clothed for it. He Gchatted me immediately and told me to tell him what I wanted to have a conversation about. I said I would tell him when we met in person and he said, "You know I have an anxiety problem, and making me wait is going to trigger the type of anxiety YOU DON'T WANT FROM ME RIGHT NOW."

I read this as clearly threatening. He was a pouty seemingly unassuming guy and a friend of a friend, which is probably why I'd kept second-guessing myself, not wanting to "overreact," but this really scared me. I gave him a really passive and overly generous summary of what I wanted to talk to him about.

We met the next night at the kitchen table. He was clothed. I was cautious, but told him I didn't think being roommates was working and I wanted him to leave. He seemed shocked. "Why?" he kept asking and acted like I was crazy. I told him some of his comments made me uncomfortable and he kept laughing, shaking his head, and acting like I was being overly sensitive. Finally, I said, "I need you to wear pants. I don't walk around in *my* underwear."

He told me, "I wouldn't care if you did. I'm cool with that."

I was visibly angry. I snapped at him. "Dude, you walked into the kitchen with a fucking erection yesterday."

"What?" He laughed. "An erection? Chavisa? Really?" He leaned forward and smirked at me. "I don't want to be mean, but that wasn't an erection. Maybe you don't really . . . know . . . you know . . . what an erection looks like?"

This was it. I told him, meanly, "I might be pretty queer, but I know what a fucking erection looks like. Your dick was moving!"

He sat back and his lip started quivering. Then he stood, paced around, and went and got his kitten and sat back down. Then, he actually started sobbing into his kitten. I mean, he pressed his face into his kitten's fur and hiccupped and sobbed.

He apologized profusely and said he didn't want to move out. He said he would start wearing pants all the time and then laid his head on the table, wept very hard, and told me that no one wanted to be around him anymore. He was fighting with his Canadian girlfriend. She wouldn't answer the phone, so he'd called her mom, and now his girlfriend was mad at him. "Was that wrong?" he asked me. "Am I just getting everything wrong?"

He came undone in a way that was difficult to watch. (I didn't feel sorry for him. I wanted to get away from him. The whole thing was pathetic and eerie.) He kept saying he didn't want to move out and would do better. It was hard, because I knew that if he didn't want to leave, I would actually have to hire a lawyer and officially evict him, which could be a tedious process that could actually cause me to lose my lease. Finally, after an hour, I agreed to let him stay. I made it clear he was to always wear pants in the common space, he wasn't allowed in my room, he shouldn't ask me for hugs anymore, or ask to go to my "lesbo parties" with me, (which he'd done a few times). I told him I don't like that word and that I didn't want to hear about his personal life and didn't want comments on mine.

He agreed, and then he said, "Okay, since this is a house meeting"—the words I'd used —"can I ask for something from *you* now?" I said he could, though I was dumbfounded by this response. "Okay, well sometimes, after you do the dishes, you leave the dishes in the drying rack and don't put them away. The drying rack is always full." I was certain, as soon as he said this, our agreement wasn't going to work. He seemed to be saying this as if it leveled the field; I had complaints about him, and he had complaints about me, also, as if these two things were equal. I told myself that the next time he did anything he'd agreed not to do, I would demand he leave, no matter what.

For the next week, he acted crazy about being overly clothed. The bathroom was right next to his room and every time he took a shower, he would stick his head out and shout loudly, "Okay, I'm coming out and going to my room now. I only have a towel on. Just warning you so you don't see me!" He did this even if I was in my room with my door closed, when there was no way I would have even seen him come out in a towel. Sometimes, I *did* see him go from the shower to his room, and he had multiple towels wrapped around his entire body, covering his shoulders and head, and he would sprint down the hall, shouting "Sorry, sorry! I know you don't want to see a naked man!" while shooting me looks that let me know he was trying to make me feel like *I* was enforcing crazy rules, though I'd never had any issue with him walking from the bathroom to his room in a towel.

Two weeks after the "house meeting," I was standing at the sink doing dishes. He came into the house, tossed his stuff down, sighed, then walked over to where I was standing and leaned against the counter, casually cornering me between the sink and the wall, blocking the only path out.

"Well, it finally happened," he said. "My girlfriend broke up with me." I glanced at him and kept washing. He was already only two feet away from me, and he took a step forward, keeping his arm on the counter, awkwardly. "I haven't had a date in forever. Maybe I should go out to some of those . . . parties with you." I rolled my eyes and sighed. He stepped forward again. "I just really need to have sex." I readied myself and scooted back, pressing into the counter behind me. He scooted forward again, so that he was a few inches away from me and pouted, looking pitiful. "I really need someone to touch my penis."

I turned and threw my hands in the air. "*Are you fucking kidding?*" I screamed. "That's it! That's fucking *it!*"

He stood up straight and looked shocked. "What? What? Oh, no. No, no, no. I don't mean *you*! Not you! Come on, that's not what I meant. You thought I meant you?" He laughed. "No, someone else. Come on."

I told him to get the fuck out of my way, pushed past him, went to my room, and locked my door. I called a straight male friend and asked him to come over and pick me up to go out. I didn't want to be alone in the house right after I told him to move out.

I went back outside. He was standing in the kitchen, arms folded, and we had a hard conversation, but I insisted he had to get out by the end of the next month. He cried a lot, sat on the floor, laid his head on the table, petted his kitten, talked about his ex-girlfriend, and told me I was being overly sensitive and taking things the wrong way. I didn't care. I wasn't going to be regularly intimidated by a man and sexually harassed in my own home.

When he'd first moved in, he'd told me that his ex-room-mate was crazy. I hadn't paid much attention to this at the time, but I have a good memory. He'd told me her first name a few times and once, casually, mentioned where she worked—a fine wine store one subway stop away. On a whim, I decided to look up his ex-roommate to get a better idea what I was dealing with.

I went to the wine store and bought a bottle of wine. No one else was in the store. I said hello to the girl checking me out and then casually asked, "Are you Michele?" (I'm using a fake name.) She said yes and I said casually, as if this was a happy coincidence, "Oh, I think you're my roommate's ex-roommate."

She looked startled. "What?" she asked, "Who?"

"Ian," I said. "He was your roommate, right?"

And the next thing she said was pretty startling for me, because she was putting up no pretense of pretending anything was in any way normal, even though I was a total stranger. She gasped and said, "Oh, no! I didn't know he was still in this neighborhood," and she looked around like he might pop up any second. Then she asked, nervously, realizing what she'd done, "Umm, I mean . . . how are things going? . . . I mean, has he been your roommate long? Like, is he staying your roommate?"

She actually asked me that. I then let all pretenses down as well and said, "No, I'm kicking him out. That's actually why I came here. I want to know if he's dangerous."

She sighed and shook her head. "Did he ever start wearing pants?"

She told me he had done the same thing with her. He seemed to be totally nice and normal when they first met. Then, after a week, stopped wearing clothing and started sleeping on the small couch in front of her bedroom door at night in nothing but his underwear.

Her boyfriend, who often stayed over, had to have a talk with him and demand that he start sleeping in his *own* room at night. This didn't work until her boyfriend finally threatened him. He said sexual things to her often, and even accused her at one point of stealing his medication from him after she asked him to move out. It was hard to get him out.

It had taken her two months, and he threatened her with legal recourse.

So, that was good to know.

* * *

In the end, I got him out, though I had to vacate my apartment for the four final days because things had gotten so toxic, I couldn't stay in my own home. When he moved out, I also found that his kitten had sprayed all the corners of his room and I had to deep clean it to get the smell out. This happened because he never wanted to get his male kitten neutered. He said it "didn't seem right to cut off his balls." I charged him a small cleaning fee, which I took out of the security deposit. He argued with me about this as well but finally relented.

I told the friend who had referred him to me everything that had happened. She sighed heavily and said, "Oh, Ian," and then, "It doesn't totally surprise me. He can be really awkward around women."

"Awkward."

Ten years later he tried to connect with me on social media. I blocked him.

69

I was twenty-nine and dressed up to go to a gala for the LGBT nonprofit I worked for. It was a costume party, a masked-ball-themed gala, and I was wearing a busty top, a long silk skirt, and an ostentatious headpiece. I was walking from the subway to the gala venue when a well-dressed man in a suit and tie began walking too closely alongside me and, I thought, looking at my chest. I picked up my pace, and he picked up his as well. "Excuse me," he said. "Excuse me. I'm sorry to bother you, I just need a little help."

"What is it?" I asked, feeling uncomfortable and keeping up a fast pace.

"I was wondering if you could help me with directions. I'm a little lost."

"Oh," I thought. "I'm being paranoid." I slowed down, nearly stopping, looked at him, and asked him where he wanted to go. Then he grabbed my breasts with both of his hands and squeezed, hard. I shoved him and ran.

70

When I was twenty-nine, I was sitting in a nice park in the West Village on my lunch break from work, eating a sandwich on a bench. A man walked up to me, leaned over me, and pulled out his penis, wagged it in my face, and told me to suck it. That was a moment when I was very thin. I weighed about 115 pounds. I was sitting, he was standing, and I felt small and helpless. I started screaming and kicking. Another man not too far away saw what was happening and started yelling, and the man ran away.

I saw where he ran to and also saw a cop on the opposite corner. I don't generally like cops, but I'd had enough. I approached the cop and told her what had happened. She told me she was off her shift, and (this was confusing) would have to call a cop who was clocked in. It would take forty-five minutes to an hour for another cop to arrive, and since the man hadn't actually touched me, there was nothing they could hold him for anyway. I went back to work.

71

When I was twenty-nine, I participated in Occupy Wall Street. I was at the park anywhere from four to six days a week for months. I was regularly sexually harassed in the crowd. I've often had conversations with leftist Marxist men who have explained to me that if we get rid of class, sexism will not be a problem.

Basically, they say that in a classless anarchist society, sexism wouldn't exist. Of course, that little enclave of OWS wasn't actually classless, but was still attempting to get as close to it as possible. Everyone lived there in tents together, sleeping in the camp through the night. After the first few weeks, many women had been sexually assaulted in the camp and a few of them had actually been raped at night.

Of course, people didn't want to report this to the police because they were already actively looking for reasons to break up the camp. OWS dealt with it anarchically, voting to separate the nighttime camp, creating one section that was optional but that was women only.

The fact that we had to do this during a social justice political protest is disgusting.

72

For six months, when I was thirty, I worked
for a small nonprofit. My boss and I were the only staff.
We worked in a donated space inside a large, posh adver-
tising agency office in midtown Manhattan. The ad agency
employed many well-dressed and good-looking young
women. My boss knew I was a lesbian and repeatedly tried to
get me to sexually harass these women with him. The women
would come over and say hello, wish us good morning, and
he would smile at them with this gross look on his face and
ask them about their day, looking them up and down as he
spoke. He would try to keep there a little too long.
When they would leave, he would ask me if I liked that girl's
ass or tits, or if I would like to sleep with her, sometimes
within earshot of the women. I barely ever even responded
to these questions, except to sometimes say, "She's not my
type," and "I think she can hear you." This never dissuaded
him in any way.

Beyond this, he would often ask my opinion, and then
completely ignore my advice about grants. I'd been grant
writing, quite successfully, for more than seven years. He'd
never written a grant in his life and I thought he had hired
me for my expertise. But he wouldn't listen to the most
basic guidance I provided, like not referring to nonprofit

services as "luxury services" with funders, who want to know the services are necessary and that their funds are being used as economically as possible.

And this is something I've often found myself wondering without a clear answer (but somewhere deep in my gut, I'm sure of the answer): "Is he discounting me as an expert because I'm a woman?"

It's sometimes not obvious and hard to explain to others compellingly why you feel certain that someone is discounting you because you're female. And if it weren't for the cumulative knowledge I have gained from an entire life lived as a woman, this might not be apparent to me either. Some men have called my certainty of not being listened to because I'm a woman "being overly sensitive because of personal experiences." I call it an informed opinion.

Because my boss knew I liked women, he treated me like a fellow "bro" when it came to being creepy to women he worked around. He also treated me like a woman, expecting emotional support from me constantly, support that I would not provide, but that he, nonetheless, imagined I was providing.

Each day, he would come in and spend about an hour telling me about his intimate and intense fights with his wife, their troubled sex life, and his issues from childhood with his father. He was my boss. The first couple of weeks, I did often try to cut him off and get back to work, but it never mattered. He was unable to take any cue—my uncomfortable sighing, my total lack of any response, my segueing into different topics. So finally, the first hour of work became his therapy session. This became my normal.

Every morning, I would sit quietly and sip my coffee while he told me about his wife breaking dishes and locking herself in the bedroom and all the horrible things they'd said to each other the night before. He alone was paying me. There was no human resources department. I sat and listened to him. I was the most silent and obviously unwilling therapist. When it came time to actually do the job he hired me for, he dismissed my ideas.

73

I was thirty, and sitting in a small art space with a prominent writer I looked up to and had had the pleasure of speaking with a handful of times over the years. We were not close friends, but he knew me well enough to be comfortable around me. He is a prominent black writer who writes about social justice, race, class, and many other political issues. In general, I respect his politics and work. I was in the room with him, an older close male friend of mine, another man who was a guest of this man, who I didn't know, and a younger male intern who worked in the art space.

We were having a conversation about the film *Precious*. The prominent writer I respected was critiquing the movie, and I agreed with and was impressed by his critiques. Mostly, I listened, until he said, "And there was no way that her father raped her. Like you could rape a girl that big, please." The needle skipped. I challenged him on this, telling him I didn't find it unbelievable that a larger (fat) woman could have been raped.

Then he clarified, saying, that it wasn't only that she was so big. It was also that she was black. He said (and I remember this word for word), "You can't rape a black woman. They'll fight you, not like a white woman."

For me, everything stopped when he said that. I got stuck on it. My mind was reeling with how to respond. I felt a rush of adrenaline and was extremely disappointed that a man I admired so much for his social and political astuteness could speak this way about women. But for the men in the room, the conversation kept going. Two of the men laughed and nodded at his statement, as if agreeing and taking in his wisdom. And then they moved on. They didn't skip a step. They found nothing strange in what he'd said. I was still processing his statement and thinking of a response, when this man asked me if I could make him some coffee.

"Oh, okay," I nodded and started to stand from my seat, then I caught myself. He and I were both guests in this space. I was sitting farthest away from the kitchen of anyone. And the much younger (also white) male intern, whose job it actually was to make visitors coffee, was sitting nearest the kitchen, but was being included in the conversation, which had moved on to the subject of how movies like *The Color Purple* are designed to paint black men as villains. I was the only woman in the room; therefore, I was the one who should make the coffee.

I sat back down in my chair. "No, I can't," I told him.
"What?"

"I can't make you a cup of coffee," I told him. "I think there's some made anyway. The pot is in the kitchen. The cups are right next to them. Maybe he" (I motioned to the intern) "could grab you a cup. He's right there."

The prominent writer gave me a horrified look. He was deeply offended. He folded his arms and said, "Well, fine."

I waited for someone else (him or the intern) to get up and get some coffee. Nothing happened. We stared at each other. He didn't get up to get any coffee. He finally started talking again, mostly to the other men. The young male intern did not even offer to go get him the coffee.

I interrupted their conversation and told him I wanted to talk about what he'd said before. He didn't seem to have any idea what I was referring to. "When you said you can't rape black women because they fight back and white women don't," I reminded him. I looked him straight in the eye and said calmly, evenly, and clearly, "That's one of the most disgusting things I've ever heard anyone say. You've equally offended black and white women in the same sentence. That's really a rare accomplishment."

Everything I did in those few minutes, those were some difficult things to do. I'd instinctively risen when he asked me to make him a cup of coffee. Maybe I'd never thought about it before. I was a woman in the room, so when asked to go make a drink or food, I always do it. Or at least, I always *had*, ever since I was a kid. This was someone much older than me, who is well-known and whom I respect and admire, and whom I also really wanted to like and respect me. Challenging him on something he said, especially when it was so complicated regarding both gender and race— because I believed it was extremely sexist and offensive to everyone he was talking about—was difficult and daunting. I had to pick my words carefully and push myself to speak. My mouth was dry as I'd said the words.

But he brushed it off. "Oh well, I'm always offending my wife and my daughter too," he told me.

I was not his wife or daughter. I was an artist he'd met in groups a few times over the last eight years, visiting a salon having a conversation about literature with other writers. But it didn't matter. I might as well have been his wife or daughter. There was an implied intimacy and obligation of servitude because I was a woman and, to him, a wife/daughter figure, but never quite a peer. All I said in response was that it didn't surprise me that his wife and daughter were often offended.

I took my bag and told all the men, coldly, that I was going to go. "So soon?" they asked.

Yes. I wasn't nice about leaving, but all the men seemed to be confused about why I was so upset. And I was upset because what he said was extremely bigoted and unfeeling, but also because this wasn't the first time a moment like this had happened in conversations with a male artist I respected. It was like the hundredth or five hundredth time. (Who's counting? Well, I guess I am, as best as I can.) But his statement was particularly jarring, grotesque, and violent. It implied a guilt of all parties spoken of, except rapists.

I had fake conversations in my head with him after, where I challenged him better, "Are all black women who claim they were raped lying?" I wanted to ask. "Do you think if women just fight back, they won't get raped or killed?" and on and on. But it didn't matter. I would never have this conversation with him, because even when I was so angry that my mouth was dry and I had to focus to keep my hands steady, he thought I was being a silly woman, emotional and overreacting.

74

I was in my early thirties and went in for a job interview at a large nonprofit organization. The supervisor and I interviewed for an hour. We had a terrific conversation. The interview had gone well and she actually told me that she wanted me to move to the final interview phase, and that I would be getting a call soon for a second interview with two other people on staff. We'd been sitting at a desk during the entire conversation, but when it was over, I stood and walked to the door and turned to shake hands with her. It was summer. I was wearing a nice dress that went down past my knees to my mid-shin, and a pair of booties. A few inches of my legs were showing, and she noticed my legs weren't shaved. What I can only describe as horror became visible on her face as she registered my unshaven legs. She blustered as she wished me goodbye.

The next day, I got a message telling me what I already knew, that I didn't get the job.

This incensed my partner at the time. When we were out, she kept relaying the story to her female, feminist friends (none of them were terribly surprised this would cause me to not get a job, nor was I), saying that perhaps every American woman (she was not American) should stop shaving their legs in solidarity with the few who choose not to. Maybe this would make it acceptable for women not to shave their legs, if everyone stopped shaving for a while.

Two of her friends responded, saying something along the lines of, "I support not shaving your legs, but I personally actually like to. It's a personal preference. It has nothing to do with feminism."

My partner responded saying, "That is what every feminist who shaves her legs says, but obviously, it is much more socially enforced than a personal preference if not shaving your legs can actually cause you to not gain employment, even at a job that requires little in-person interaction with anyone."

I thought she had a good point.

75

This one is for the hundreds of times men have grabbed my waist in a crowd and moved me aside. Total strangers taking hold of my waist with both hands and moving me to the side to get around me in a crowded event or space. I do not see men grab other men by the waist and move them. I hate when they do this.

76

I was in my early thirties and was at a lesbian bar
in the West Village. A woman began flirting with me. Her
friend was with her. They were both black. The girl who was
flirting with me eventually asked me if I wanted to go home
with her. I agreed. I really liked her.

Throughout the night there had been a couple walking
around—a white man and white woman approaching
women at the dyke bar, asking if we would like to have a
threesome with them.

They'd asked me. I'd told them I thought they should
leave, which pissed the man off. They were being annoying
about the whole thing. The man, without so much as a hello,
just walked up to many women and told us that his girlfriend was giving him a threesome as a birthday present and
then asked if we would fuck them. They were acting like this
bar was a lesbian zoo.

I was getting picked up and taken home by a woman
who'd actually had a good conversation with me for a couple
of hours. She'd flirted with me, which is what I hope for
when I go to the dyke bar; not to be tapped on the shoulder
by straight couples as they make their way down a row of
women, like I'm some sideshow freak performing lesbian sex
tricks. I don't know what to compare this behavior to, but it

wasn't the first time I'd encountered a straight couple doing this very thing at a gay bar, so I'd put them out of my mind.

The woman who was picking me up, her friend, and I were walking out of the crowded bar and this straight couple was standing in front of the doorway, the only exit. I said, "Excuse me, we need to get by," and tapped the man on the shoulder.

The man turned and snapped, "Wait a second!" We waited a few seconds, and they continued their conversation, not moving aside. The girl I'd been flirting with tried to scoot her way around them. As she did so, a zipper on the woman's purse snagged on her jacket and I guess it pulled at the purse, and the woman started yelling at her boyfriend, "She's trying to steal my purse! She's trying to steal my purse!"

The man turned and started yelling at us and cussing. "What are you bitches doing?" He grabbed his girlfriend's purse and tugged so that my new date got pulled with it. She had her hand on the purse zipper, because she was trying to unlatch her jacket, but the woman kept smacking her hand and yelling, "She's trying to steal my purse!" It was ridiculous. This straight white woman was screaming at a black lesbian in a dyke bar and smacking her for "trying to steal her purse." Please. Finally, my friend got unlatched and pushed her way toward the door. I cussed at the straight couple, "What the fuck is wrong with you?" and the man flipped me off, holding his finger up to my face. "Fuck you, you fucking bitch," he told me.

I don't know what came over me. Maybe it was the idea of being called a bitch by a straight man in a dyke bar that pushed me over the edge, or the fact that they were racist pieces of shit, or both.

The girls I was leaving with later said that I got this extremely calm and blank look on my face, and then I grabbed his middle finger (which he was holding up to my face), hard, gripping his finger totally in my fist, and started bending it backwards, far backwards. He started screaming and moving with his finger. His whole body, I suddenly realized, could be controlled by manipulating just one finger. When he was on his knees, I let go of him and turned and walked out.

They followed us outside and started yelling at the doorman. He told the bouncer that I had broken his finger and that we'd tried to steal her purse, and he and his girl-friend were also shouting at the woman I was going on a date with calling her and her friend animals: "You fucking animals tried to steal my purse! You're animals! Animals!"

They said this word a lot and it definitely had a racist edge to it.

We laughed at them, mocking them from across the street, then walked around the corner, got into the car, and drove away.

This wasn't the first time and it wouldn't be the last that a man and sometimes a man and a woman came into the dyke bar and tried to solicit sex from the women there in a rude and, not even remotely smooth, manner and ended up causing a scene doing it.

People pick each other up at bars; I get that. But straight, cis men, a dyke bar is not a place for you to come, walk around, tap women on the shoulder one after another and ask, without so much as a hello, if we would like to fuck you. Seriously?

77

I've realized most people assume, that as a writer, I'm the one who chooses the images that accompany my work in magazines and on the covers of my books. For the most part, this is not true. I often have no control over the images that accompany my work. Sometimes, I don't even see the images until the work is published. Other times, I have some input, but not the final vote. And I'm not going to single out any one publisher here, because this has happened with innumerable magazines and presses.

But this is what happens: I have a story published that has nothing to do with anything sexual, includes no sexy or feminine female characters, and the image accompanying the story is a woman in lingerie, in a sexual position, or I am presented with images of young girls, in short skirts and fishnets, looking slightly punk (perhaps they think that's a tie-in). If I push back, I am labeled a diva or accused of being overly sensitive.

Once, I finally found words to convey my distaste to a man in charge of the aforementioned brand of image. I said to him, after seeing the umpteenth image of a teenage girl in a skirt, "I don't understand this. If I were a man, and I wrote a story that had nothing to do with feminine teenage girls, literally had no feminine teenage girls in it, would you be suggesting a cover design of a fourteen-year-old girl's legs sticking out from beneath lacy skirts? This doesn't make any sense."

He looked thoughtful and actually said out loud, "What would I do if you were a man? Okay." I finally got an image I loved. I think he finally heard me. I think this one man finally understood. And that was the most relieving thing because every time this happens I feel demoralized.

I can't get away from this in everyday life and I accept that, but I am actually more protective of the integrity of my art than I am of myself. When sexism cuts deep enough that it starts to bleed into and mar my art, that is too much for me. That is the only time I actually start to feel hopeless.

78

I was thirty and was on my lunch break from work. I went to a nearby park and sat down in the grass in an open meadow. I took out a book and began reading while eating my sandwich. This was an open area and I was the only one sitting on the grass. There was plenty of space.

A traditionally handsome, well-dressed young white man, I would guess in his mid-twenties, walked up to me and stood over me. "You look peaceful," he told me. I nodded.

"It's a nice day," I responded politely.

He asked, "Can I sit with you?" and then began to sit down right next to me on the open lawn.

"Oh, no," I said. "No." But he was already sitting right next to me, so close that our elbows were touching.

He seemed perplexed, "Wait, did you say no?"

I nodded, placing my book in my lap. "Yes, I said no. I really just want to be alone and read my book."

"You told me I can't sit here?" he said aggressively, as if this were an unbelievable thought.

"I really just want to be alone," I told him, expecting him to apologize and get up and leave. But instead, he persisted.

"I only want to talk to you," he said.

"I don't want to talk," I said.

"Wow, you're rude!" he said.

I stared at him, annoyance visible in my expression. His lips were parted and he was looking at me like I was an unbelievable person. He was a good-looking young white man relaxing in a park in midtown. He was well-dressed enough that I supposed he had some money and as he stared at me, I realized that he probably had not heard "no" many times in his life, especially not from a woman he was expressing interest in. Who was I, anyway?

"I really just want to eat my lunch and read my book," I said, exhaustion notable in my voice. "I'm on my lunch break."

"Fine," he said. Then he turned slightly away from me and pulled his legs to his chest, wrapped his arms around his legs, and rested his head on his knees like a pouting child. He was still so close he was touching me. He sat there, next to me, up against me, glaring into the distance. I sighed, gathered my things, put my sandwich back into my bag, put my book away, and left.

He glared at me as I left, like I was doing something unbelievably rude. I went back into the office, finishing my lunch at my desk, angry that I couldn't even enjoy thirty minutes to sit alone in the park and take in the sunlight.

79

I was thirty and babysitting for a friend. On the walk
to his house, I was catcalled several times by multiple men,
whistling at me, saying, "Hey sexy," and "Hey gorgeous,
can I get your number?" then calling me a bitch or yelling,
"What's your problem?" when I ignored them. All of this is
a normal experience when walking down a populated street,
alone, as a woman, and something I've grown used to.

I went and picked up the baby. I folded her in a swad-
dling cloth and carried her against my chest. I walked the
exact same path back from where I'd come, toward a baby-
friendly café, and this time, with the baby in my arms, no
men harassed me at all. One of them said, "Good morning,
missus. What a lovely mother and baby," and another man
actually saluted me as I passed.

Yeah. Saluted me.

I guess I'd finally done my duty as a woman.

Okay.

80

When I was thirty, my second book was published by a fairly well-known press that is distributed by a major publisher.

Repeatedly, the reaction from men who learned that I had a book coming out from this press was not, "Congratulations!" or "What's your book about?" but "Oh, wow. They're publishing *your* book. Well, maybe that means they would publish *mine*."

Now, maybe these male writers were just assholes. Maybe they would have responded that way to other men. But I do think this is gendered behavior because a woman has never responded that way to this statement. Not to me.

There are interactions almost every woman has where we walk away with this glaring question inside us that is, for all practical purposes, ultimately unanswerable: "Did he treat me that way because I'm a woman?"

For me, this question has most often arisen around interactions I've had with men speaking about my writing.

I've had this experience dozens of times, but the most glaring example of this was with a young man I met through Steve Cannon.

I met this young man while visiting A Gathering of the Tribes. I'd only met this man in person once or twice before and had barely ever spoken to him.

When I came in, Steve told me congratulations and told the young man, "You gotta tell her congratulations. She got her book picked up by Seven Stories Press."

"Oh really?" He leaned forward and said, "Wow. They're publishing your book?" He looked thoughtful. "Maybe they'll publish mine then. I've been working on this book for years and can't find a publisher." Then he went straight into telling me the entire plot of his novel in progress. This took about ten minutes. When he was done, he asked again if I thought my press would publish his book.

I was pretty stunned and said, "I don't know. You can submit it to them, like anyone else can. They primarily publish work with social and political themes, though." (His book was about a man who'd been broken up with by a girl he really loved, and then went and spent a long time alone in a shack in a desert writing.)

He then asked, "Would you mention my book to the press?"

This was extremely odd since: 1.) I'd never read his writing, at all. 2.) My book hadn't even been published yet, and I was in no position to be calling in favors. If I ever did mention a book to my press, it would definitely be for a writer I actually knew and had a relationship with and whose work I believed in. 3.) I couldn't believe he still didn't even have the basic decency to ask anything about my book before asking for a rather large and nonsensical favor.

I told him didn't know if I could do that, but if he wanted, I would take a look at his book. I was being polite because he was a volunteer for Steve, but as soon as I said it I regretted it. I visited with Steve a bit longer and this man also stayed and visited, occasionally talking about how smart but underappreciated he was, and eventually I left.

Three days later, I received an email from this man, telling me he had taken my advice and sent his novel in to the press that was publishing me. He'd sent it to the attention of the director of the press with a letter stating that *I had recommended him* and his book to the press, and that his novel was attached to this email if I wanted to read it.

I was completely blown away. He'd used *my name* to my publisher, claiming I endorsed a manuscript I hadn't even read, all without my permission.

I sent him an angry email back, and he responded saying Steve had told him to do it. I confronted Steve, and he said the man had kept talking about it after I left, and Steve had simply told him to submit his book to the press or to send me his novel and see if I liked it and would put a word in.

I sent another email to the man telling him what Steve had said and also asking, "Even if Steve had told you to do this, why would you think you shouldn't check with me before using my name? Why would you think I would endorse a book I haven't even read one word of?"

I contacted my editor and told her what had happened, and she told me she would alert the interns and the director and that they would throw the manuscript away. (I hadn't asked for her to do this, but just to make sure the director knew that this man was using my name without my permission, but she insisted and I no longer cared what happened to his manuscript.)

I don't want to be an angry feminist. I want to write books and be part of a vibrant community of artists, hopefully garnering some respect from artists around me. But it seems, in order to do that, I have to be an angry feminist. And again, though this is more of a gray area, it sure felt like gendered behavior to me. The message was, I'm a woman, so I exist to be a conduit for "serious" male artists. Like, if a press is publishing *my* book then the bar must be set low and they would *definitely* publish a man's book, right?

81

I was thirty-one and at a local neighborhood bar in Bushwick with a female friend who was in her mid-twenties. We were having a nice night out, playing pool and catching up. The pool lineup paired us with two young men who were part of a small group of guys visiting New York City from Ireland. This was the first or second year I'd really started seeing tourists in Bushwick. I found it odd. Whatever.

We were playing pool with these two Irish boys and one of them, each time he hit a ball into the pocket, started walking up to my younger female friend, placing the pole between his legs, pretending it was a giant dick, and humping the air, shouting "Woohoo! Yeah! Ball in the hole." He was humping at her, and she kept telling him to cut it out. The third time he did this, she screamed at him, and I stepped up and told him to leave her the fuck alone.

He walked away, then she went to the table and when she bent over to take her shot, he hopped back over and stuck his pool stick up her skirt, goosing her from behind.

I grabbed him and punched him once. When he turned back to me, I shoved him so hard, he flew three feet back, hit the wall and then fell over, landing hard on his ass on the floor.

A ruckus ensued, mostly consisting of his friends standing between us, telling me they were protecting me from him, and me chiding them, asking if they were sure it wasn't the other way around. "Let him come over here if he can. He's still on the fucking ground."

My friend and I ended up leaving to get away from them, but I really thought they should have been kicked out.

82

I was thirty-two, riding the subway to the airport with my girlfriend. She was leaving and I wasn't going to see her for a while, so we were kissing and cuddling, being sentimental and affectionate.

A physically imposing, middle-aged man who was standing by the door was glaring at us. We stopped cuddling and sat more rigidly, now only holding hands. He stood up and walked over to us, holding on to the pole above us and leaning over, so there was no way we could get up and get away. He was well over six feet tall, sturdily built, broad, and muscular.

He told us that we were sick dykes and that he was going to rape us.

He then began asking other men on the subway to rape us with him.

"Who'll rape these ugly dykes with me? Who'll take one of them?"

He asked this loudly for four or five stops, going on about how we weren't natural women, how weird we looked, and how he was going to "rape us straight" graphically.

I was terrified. My girlfriend was terrified. All the seats on the subway were full. Everyone on the subway sat and stared. No one did anything.

We are usually much less affectionate in public now.

83

I was thirty-two. It was Halloween and I was wearing a busty witch costume. I was with a male friend at a diner after a costume party. I stepped outside and saw a group of men and women smoking and chatting. I realized I was out of cigarettes and approached the group and asked if one of them could spare a cigarette. A man in the group stepped close to me, looked me up and down, and said, "Sure, if I can suck on your breasts."

I said, "What the fuck?" He repeated it louder, as if perhaps I hadn't actually heard him.

84

I was thirty-three, shooting a music video with a friend and a group of fellow artists. My costume for this was busty and revealing. There was a fully naked man on the set and most people were in different states of near undress in various weird costumes. We were all artists or actors. We were shooting a still, silent, tableau scene.

I was standing facing a man I didn't know, who was a friend of a friend. I had to stand close to him for the tableau. He kept staring at my chest and, finally, he leaned in and whispered, "Are your breasts bigger than your head?"

"What?" I yelled loudly, so that everyone on the set could hear. "Did you ask me if my breasts are bigger than my head?" All the other actors turned and stared at him.

His face paled. "No, no, no." He whispered to me, "I'm sorry. I'm sorry."

Then the director stepped in from another room and shouted for us to get on our marks. Everyone looked away, readying themselves, and we shot the scene. When it was over, we all stayed around to clean up and have a breakdown party, but he left immediately, too embarrassed to stay and mingle.

85

I was thirty-three. I was leaving my job at a nonprofit that is dedicated to stopping anti-LGBTQ bullying in K–12 schools. The office is located on Wall Street in the financial district. I was dressed butch, with a freshly shaved head, in a collared shirt, vest, and tie.

Three typical Wall Street–looking guys in their mid- to late twenties were standing on the corner. They had probably just left happy hour at a nearby bar.

They turned and saw me coming down the street and started laughing and clapping their hands. One of them started saying, "You're beautiful. You're so pretty," obviously meaning this sarcastically.

I tried to ignore them and walk around them, but this man blocked my path, grabbed me by the back of my head and said, "Let's get drunk and make out, sweetheart."

Then he forcibly French-kissed me, mostly licking my mouth. I began punching him and I landed one good punch in the middle of his chest, because he had me by the back of my head and our heads were too close together, so I couldn't get a good punch in his face. When I landed that hit in his chest, he jumped back, and I swung again and missed. He started screaming for me to calm down and kept laughing, "Calm down, sweetheart."

I screamed at him not to fucking touch me. He told me, "I would never touch you. You're fucking ugly." Of course, he had just sexually assaulted me.

Honestly, after that I stopped dressing so butch so often. A few days later I even threw away the new collared shirt I'd been wearing.

86

I was thirty-four, visiting Southern Illinois. A drunk
man started sexually harassing me and my friends, including
one of my male friends at a bar. He was being pushy and
handsy. He was extremely intoxicated. He kept grabbing my
shoulders, trying to French-kiss me as well as my male friend
and asking if he could have a threesome with us. My friend
(who is gay, but sometimes we're not out at every moment in
Southern Illinois) told him I was his girlfriend and to leave
me alone. He also told the man that the other girl was his
younger sister. (She actually was.) Yet he persisted.

He kept trying to get to my friend's sister, but we wouldn't
let him and when I put myself between him and her, he
tried to make out with me instead. I shoved him lightly and
hollered to the bartender that I needed this man to leave us
alone. (We were just trying to have a beer and catch up after
not seeing each other for more than a year.) The bartender
yelled at him.

He went and sat back down in his seat, then ten minutes
later, came over to apologize. But while he was apologizing,
he kept trying to get too close to my friend's little sister
again. I placed myself between him and her, again, and then
he grabbed my breasts with both of his hands and squeezed.

I shoved him, and he fell back and hit the wall. I put my

hand on his chest, raised my fist, and yelled loudly at him, telling him that if he touched me again, I was going to beat the shit out of him.

He left the bar, then came back fifteen minutes later and asked me and my friends to make out with him. Then the bartender finally had him permanently removed.

87

I was thirty-four. I was talking to a man at a house party, a birthday party of my close friend. It was August and extremely hot in a crowded apartment with no air-conditioning and many people had taken off layers of clothing. I was down to an undershirt/tank top. I had put on some weight for various reasons and was now a size fourteen.

I didn't know this man well, but I'd met him with other friends a few times before.

He started complimenting my looks and told me I was brave to be so "out there" with my wild hair and punky clothes.

He then clarified what he meant by brave. "Most women of your build would hide."

88

I was thirty-four, visiting the southern, rural Midwest, which was the farm-town area where I was born and raised. I was spending time with my younger female cousin. She was twenty-seven at the time. We went to a local bar and had two drinks, with food, over the course of about two hours.

A man was talking to us for quite a while, hovering around us, and kept asking if he could buy either of us a drink. He was hitting on my cousin persistently, even though she was barely responding to his come-ons.

The young man was badly dressed. He was wearing an old T-shirt and dusty blue jeans with tattered cuffs. My cousin smiled awkwardly and nodded when he talked to her, then repeatedly turned and tried to talk to me to get out of the conversation with him. We walked away from him and went and sat at a table on the patio. He followed us over and stood next to my cousin after she took a seat. He told her, "I'm in really good shape," and patted his abs. Then he said, "I used to be in better shape, but I can't work out as much since I injured my foot."

She nodded and asked meekly, "Oh? How did you hurt it?"

"Kicked a mailbox," he responded. My cousin and I both suppressed laughter. This young man was a poor country boy and we didn't want to badly insult him. But we still wished he would leave.

I needed to use the bathroom and get another drink. I told my cousin I was going inside for a minute. The young man asked me if he could buy me a drink, again. I declined, again. He then asked my cousin, again, if he could buy her a drink. She declined, again. "I'm still drinking my drink," she said, motioning to her vodka and Coke, which was almost totally full. He persisted and asked her again if he could buy her one when she was finished. "No." She declined, again.

I thought this was strange, but mostly it registered to me in that moment as masculine pomp. I thought he thought if he bought one of us a drink, my cousin would owe him something. I went in and used the restroom, got a second drink, and when I came back out, my cousin was surrounded. Three of the young man's friends were all standing around her where she sat at the table, leaning over her, chatting her up. She seemed overwhelmed. I came and sat next to her and effectively shooed them away.

About twenty minutes later, when she was nearly finished with her second vodka soda, she began acting oddly. She'd only consumed two drinks in a two-hour priod, but seemed confused. When she stood to walk, she stumbled, and when I grabbed hold of her arm to balance her, she turned, grabbed me by my shoulders, and asked me where we were and how we'd gotten there. She didn't remember coming to the bar. She'd been at this bar several times before over the years, but she didn't even recognize where she was.

We were having mixed drinks, the second being very light, and I knew she could handle more than two, especially spaced out and with food. But at first, I thought maybe hers had been an exceptionally strong drink. She was young and small, and I wasn't sure what was going on. I took her away from the bar. We left and went to a store, where I got her some water and another snack. She drank the water and ate half a slice of pizza, but she didn't get better. She didn't even remember our drive from the bar to the store. She was awake, but she was continuously confused and acting strangely. Rather than beginning to sober up as time passed, she was getting worse. After another hour, she began vomiting profusely, and I finally realized she had been roofied, most likely by the young man who was coming on to her and pushing to buy us drinks at the bar.

Whatever he put in her drink lasted for about six hours, and she has little memory of the entire night. This man drugged her against her consent and stole our time together, which we'd both really been looking forward to, since we don't get to see each other often.

This man poisoned her with the hope of raping her. He didn't get to rape her, but he still poisoned her. She still had to deal with the effects on her body and psyche.

89

I was thirty-three and at a dyke bar in the West Village with my girlfriend and some other female friends. There was a tall straight man there who was walking around the bar and hitting on all of us. I was dressed more butch that day, and my girlfriend was dressed more femme. I was a few feet away from my girlfriend, who was dancing with our other female friends, and this tall straight man approached her and tried to dance with her, but not the kind of casual dancing she'd been doing. He tried to take her by the hand and waist and tried to pull her close to him. She stepped back and shook her head no. Yet he persisted.

I didn't go over or step in then, because other girlfriends have told me when I do that it makes them feel infantilized, as if they can't handle themselves in public. So, I did my best to hold back and just stay watchful.

He kept talking to her, leaning down, and then took hold of her shoulder. She pulled away and made a beeline for me. She came and stood on the other side of me and told me this guy wouldn't leave her alone and she didn't want to deal with it anymore. Okay.

I said, "Let's stay over here for a minute," thinking he would forget about her, but of course, he came over to us and started berating her for being rude, saying he only wanted to dance with her. Why wouldn't she dance with him?

I was in between them. He actually reached over me to try to touch her at one point and I put my hand in the air, blocking him from taking her by the shoulder again. I told him, "She doesn't want to dance with you. This is a dyke bar. Why are you even here?"

He said he was there with a female friend, claimed she was bisexual, and that he had as much right to be here as anyone. I said, "Okay, whatever. Just leave us alone." Then I took my girlfriend's hand and walked her around him, myself between him and her, and headed back to the other side of the crowded bar, my girlfriend in front of me. As I was almost to the other side of the bar, I felt this man shoulder-check me from behind, hard. I lurched forward. He said, "Move, lesbot!"

I've never actually been called a "lesbot" before. And this was in a dyke bar. I didn't even think about it. I turned and shoved him hard and he toppled over, hitting his head on the wall and falling down through the crowd onto the floor. I started shouting that he'd shoved me and repeated, "You're going to call me a lesbot in a gay bar? Seriously?"

Five big butch women stood up from where they had been sitting and got in between him and me, taking hold of him as he got back up and was turning to face me. This bar was crowded, shoulder to shoulder. People started yelling for him to get out, and someone must have gotten the bouncer, because the bouncer quickly came in and got hold of the man and began walking him out of the bar. The man was pleading his case and I heard the bouncer, who was also a straight man, say to this man, "I know, I know. But they're all upset. You know how they are."

About fifteen minutes later, my friends and I decided we needed a cigarette and went outside to smoke. I thought the man would have been long gone by now, but after we lit up, we saw that he was still arguing with the doorman on the other side of the door. His female friend was with him and she saw us and started squealing at the doorman, "You mean you'll let *them* back in, but not *us*? Are you kidding me?"

She then looked at my butch friend and actually started making fun of what she was wearing. "Look at you, you're ugly. What are you wearing? Cargo pants?" She said something degrading about her button-up shirt and tie. "And that fucking giant key chain? What's wrong with you?" Then she laughed. (Yes, she actually mocked a butch's ring of keys at a dyke bar.) Then she said to my friend, "What are you, like, forty?!" as if someone being forty was outrageous.

My friend responded loudly, "Yes, I'm forty-two!"

We put out our cigarettes early and went back into the dyke bar, leaving them out there, arguing with the doorman.

I was thirty-four. I was walking down the street with my girlfriend and her teenage daughter. We are all queer and punky-looking. As we were walking, a man who was coming in our direction saw us, stopped, stepped into the middle of the sidewalk and blocked our path, shouting, "Look at these fat ugly bitches. I would like to kill these fat ugly bitches. What horrible ugly women you are."

We had to cross the street to get around him. He kept shouting after us as we hurried away.

A few days after the 2016 presidential election, I was walking in midtown, holding hands with my girlfriend, and a man ran up to us, threw his hand in the air in a Nazi salute and began shouting, "TRUMP, TRUMP, TRUMP." Then he got close behind us, and began pantomiming humping each of us, shouting "DYKES!!! DYKES! Trump! Trump! Trump!"

92

I was at the first Women's March in New York City. My partner and I had spent the day walking in the protest. It was dusk, and we'd reached the end of the march. Exhausted, we went a few blocks away, stood near a ledge in an all-but-empty Bryant Park, and began checking our phones for messages from friends we were supposed to meet after the march, looking for a nearby place where we could rest and eat.

Our signs were lying on the ground beside us. It was obvious we'd come from the massive protest, which was still happening a few blocks away.

While I was looking at my phone, a man body slammed me from behind. It sent a shooting pain down my back and was hard enough to cause me to lurch forward.

He walked around us, turned, and laughed and sneered at us. He was a well-dressed, rich-looking white man in his late twenties. He was walking with a woman who seemed to be his date, who was wearing a nice dress and heels. She was glaring at me and my partner. It was obvious to me that they were both Trump supporters.

I started yelling at him, and he turned and stood a few feet away and glared at me. I ran up to him but stopped short, realizing that if I hit him back, and the police were called, they would almost definitely arrest me, not him.

I was wearing all black, had been protesting all day, and looked like a disheveled anarchist, and he was a superrich resident of this Manhattan neighborhood. I spit in his face. He stared at me like he wanted to kill me, then smirked, turned, and walked away casually.

93

When I was thirty-five, I was at a bar with a straight male friend who had, about a year before, made objectifying offhand comments about my and my lover's bodies, comparing and contrasting how sexy different parts of our body were. "She has a better ass, but you have better tits." After those comments, I argued with him, but he didn't take me seriously, so I stopped speaking to him for several months. He finally asked me why I didn't like him anymore and I told him, clearly, that I didn't want to be friends with a man who talked that way to me and my partner.

"We're not in competition with each other to be more attractive to men. I don't care what you think about my body sexually and I don't want to hear about it."

We had a long conversation with my girlfriend. He actually listened and apologized profusely.

I had known him for more than ten years, and really care about him, and I accepted his apology.

Months later I was talking to him at a bar. I began walking away to go get a drink and he smacked my ass. I turned and told him that I wasn't cool with that, and that I didn't want him to touch my ass again. We were surrounded by other straight men at the bar. They were watching this interaction. He looked embarrassed and explained to me that he wasn't smacking my ass sexually. That it was a friendly joke.

I told him that I didn't care what his intentions were. It's my body and I have the right to tell him not to do that if I don't like it and he has to listen. "Just don't do it again, okay?"

He said, "Oh, come on. This?" and smacked my ass again.

I left the bar and didn't speak to him for several months. He finally apologized for that too. And no, it's not like having a man I know smack my ass is a horribly traumatic experience. It was just unwanted and I didn't like it. And I get to define how people touch my body, especially if that touching has an intimate or sexual overtone. That's it. And if they don't listen to me, that's offensive and demeaning. Anyway, he apologized again and now, because we are often in the same place, I speak to him if I run into him, but I do feel on guard.

94

A few days after I wrote that last chapter,
about this friend of mine, there was another incident with
this same friend.

There's a local bar/coffeehouse a few blocks away from
my house, which I frequent often. I spend most days alone
at home writing in isolation. So I really enjoy having a place
I can walk to at the end of the day where I can interact
with people I know, some well and some casually, have a
drink, and relax in the three-dimensional company of other
humans.

I think this is a pretty normal thing to want to do. But
sometimes it's difficult for me to do this because I'm a woman.

So anyway, a few days after I wrote that last chapter, I
had spent the day inside working. It was nine o'clock and
I decided to go have a drink at my local bar outside in the
patio section. I saw this old friend of mine (the one from the
previous chapter) outside talking to another man. I said hello
and as I was attempting to put down my bag and drink, my
friend introduced me to this man he was sitting with.

I introduced myself and reached out and shook this man's
hand. The man introduced himself and started talking,
but was not letting go of my hand even though I was done
shaking his. I was pulling away, and was in an awkward

position with my bag hanging from my arm and my drink in the other hand.

This interaction was strange and quick. I tugged on my hand a second time and he squeezed my hand harder, not letting go of it, and kept talking.

I tugged on my hand a third time and he squeezed so hard that it actually hurt my fingers and pulled me toward him. I said, "Excuse me, can I have my hand back?"

He didn't let go, so I yanked my hand so hard that he actually lurched forward when I pulled, and finally I got my hand free from his grip. I sat my bag and drink down and stared at the man in confusion.

He was looking at me angrily. He told me that I was rude.

I simply asked, "Why wouldn't you let go of my hand? That was fucked up."

He told me that I was being rude and that he's from Africa and that it's normal for people in Africa to hold hands when they talk. I said it's not normal anywhere to keep holding on to someone's hand after they pull away from you and ask for their hand back. I told him that I have friends from all over the world, including Africa, but I didn't know it was normal anywhere to squeeze a woman's hand like that when she wants you to let go of her.

He said, "This isn't about me being a man and you being a woman. This is about me being African and you being American."

I came back angrily with, "Really? If you were shaking a *man's* hand and he wanted it back, you would have clamped down like that and not let go? Oh, please. Give me a fucking break."

Then, my friend, who I've known for a long time, rolled his eyes, stood up from where he was sitting and said, "This conversation is boring!" Then he laughed weirdly and turned and reached for my breasts with both of his hands in a breast-honking motion.

His hands barely touched the front of both of my breasts, just barely making contact with the front of my shirt, about a centimeter away from really landing down, because I immediately jumped back.

I yelled, "What the fuck are you doing?" He was left standing there with his hands held out in the air like a cartoon character preparing to squeeze two tits. I didn't really think about it. I punched him in the chest.

My body is not fodder for relief from male boredom. After he recovered from the punch and everyone gasped, he told me that he wasn't going for my breasts, that he was going for my shoulders and had miscalculated his aim.

I was thunderstruck by all of this. I couldn't even go to a bar and relax, chat, and have a drink. I don't even mind people flirting with me. That's *fine*. I expect some amount of flirting at a bar. But this was not flirting. Literally, within *two minutes* of my arrival, two men had invaded my body in sexist and aggressive ways and immediately after, told me that it had nothing to do with my being a woman.

I had this feeling of being a small animal walking into a feeding frenzy and being ravaged, when all I wanted to do was have casual conversation and relax after a long day.

I told my friend that what he'd done was unacceptable and that I was done with him and walked away.

The next day he sent me a series of text messages apologizing to me and telling me that he'd meant to put his hands on my chest, to jokingly shove me, which of course was different than what he'd said before, but I know when someone is about to grab my breasts and squeeze them, especially when their hands are a centimeter away from gripping each of my breasts. It was obvious.

He continued insisting that wasn't what he was going to do, and of course there's always this question in my head, "Am I being overdramatic? Was I mistaken? Am I making a big deal out of something that isn't a big deal?" No matter how obvious it is, when a man I know tells me something sexist that obviously happened didn't happen, I *still* question myself. I feel guilty, and also like maybe this is going to make all other men I'm friends with hate me or fear me or not want to be around me.

But this wasn't even the first time he'd done something like this, or the second or the fifth or sixth. And I think that a lot of men fail to understand that this is not fun for me to write. It's not fun or exciting for me to be mad at him. I don't want this attention. I don't want to burn him at the stake.

I am really sad that in order to have respect for myself, I can no longer be friends with him. I miss him. I really cared about him. I liked our friendship. I'm sad to lose it.

He'd done a lot of really generous and helpful things for me over the years. This friendship was good for me in many ways. There are ways that he made my life easier. And also, I really liked being able to have an old friend, someone I've known for more than ten years, at a place that I often visit so near my home. In New York City, this was rare and pleasant.

This is sad for me. I hate that I can't be friends with him anymore and if I really thought that I was mistaken and that this wasn't a big deal, I would probably do everything I could to sweep it away, as I did so many other things he's done. But I can't anymore. Because the next time he does something, it will probably be worse than the last thing he did and I would only have myself to blame, right? I should've known better?

That's a double-edged sword of sexism. If I respond to this sort of repeated behavior and draw a line, I am seen as making a big deal out of nothing. If I don't respond to it and something worse happens to me, I should've known better.

And one of the saddest parts of this for me is that I will actually miss his company and I know he thinks I'm being melodramatic.

95

I was thirty-five. I was walking home from a Fourth of July party. In New York City, the Fourth of July is a pretty big public celebration and a lot of people revel in the streets drunkenly. I have noticed, though, that all over the world, whenever there's a loud, drunken, public celebration, it can't just be joyful and Dionysian, but it seems women have to bear the brunt of drunken, aggressive male behavior.

I was walking down the sidewalk and a man stepped in front of me and said, "Hey, baby! Hey, beautiful. Hey!" I did not respond but kept walking. He then told me, "Okay, mama, bless you." Then shouted aggressively and loudly, "I *said*, bless you!"

I went into the deli to get a bottle of water and some snacks. I stood next to another woman in line. A group of drunk young men came in. While we were waiting in line, one man picked his friend up in a bear hug and began swinging him around, knocking his body into the woman who was standing next to me. She was in her mid-twenties and probably weighed a hundred pounds. The men were much larger than her. She had as little reaction as possible after recovering from being knocked forward into the counter. She stood aside and we both just looked down, avoiding eye contact with this group of men. "Damn man, be careful," one man said.

"I don't give a fuck," the man who'd done the swinging replied (speaking of the young woman).

That woman paid and left. I stepped up to pay. As I was waiting for my change, one of the men (older than the others) said, "Hello, beautiful," directed at me. I did not respond, but kept facing forward. He stepped up and put his body next to mine, leaning in and put his face directly in front of my face, and repeated, more loudly and aggressively this time, "Did you hear me? I just gave you a compliment. Hello! Beautiful!" He said loudly. I didn't respond.

"Oh you're scared. You're scared of us, huh?" he said, and they all began laughing.

I turned and said, snapping in anger, "I'm not fucking scared. I'm just completely tired of this shit."

The older man stepped back and said, "All right, all right."

I took my change. His young friend hopped up and followed me out the door. He screamed, "Welcome to Brooklyn, bitch."

I've lived here for fifteen years.

96

I was thirty-five, and I was on a day date with my
girlfriend near Pike Place Market in Seattle. I was dressed up
for our date and had slicked my hair over. My girlfriend and
I stopped into a corner store to grab a couple of small things:
a bottle of water, a pack of gum, and cigarettes. When I
stepped up to the counter, the male cashier's eyes lit up. I
sat my purchases on the counter for him to ring up, but he
didn't do anything. He just stared at me and smiled brightly.

"You are very beautiful," he told me. "Very, very beautiful.
And strange. It's different. Different look. I love your hair.
Very beautiful." English was his second language and he
spoke with an accent.

I just pursed my lips and nodded, pushing my things forward. This was the only store that sold cigarettes for several
blocks. I asked him for a pack of cigarettes. He turned and
grabbed them, then stood at the counter, holding them and
staring at me.

"I like having style too," He said. "I keep my hair nice.
Very clean, like you. You're very beautiful. I keep my hair
nice. I put oil in it. Olive oil to make it shine like this." He
motioned to his hair like he was a spokesmodel for himself.
"It smells good and keeps it very shiny," he told me. Then,
he leaned forward, placing the top of his head in front of my

face and said, "You can smell it." He said this as if he were allowing me to do something I was obviously just dying to do.

I laughed lightly and looked to my girlfriend, who had a giant grin on her face, her mouth open in awe of what was happening. "No, thank you," I told him.

"What?" he said, shocked and stood back up. "It's clean! I keep clean. Go ahead and smell it. It smells good."

"Nah, I'm good," I said. "I just want the cigarettes."

"But my hair smells good," he kept on. I shook my head no. He finally rang me up and said, "Maybe I take you out sometime? I keep clean and nice."

I said no again, took my things, and left the store.

Sometimes sexual harassment is tedious, and sometimes it's traumatic, and sometimes it's just so insane that it's hilarious.

"You can smell it" has become a beloved and hilarious catchphrase between my girlfriend and me. "I think this has gone bad. Okay. You can smell it." Or, "Do you like my new haircut?" (bending over) "You can smell it!"

Amazing.

97

I was thirty-five and visiting home (the rural, southern Midwest). I'd met some friends from high school at a local pub. We spent the night having food and drinks and catching up. People really mingle at this particular establishment and most people here know each other. It's a popular small-town bar with snacks, which often hosts karaoke and live music. People are friendly. One of my friends had introduced me to a man my age earlier in the night and we'd hit it off and shared some jokes. I enjoyed his conversation. My friend had introduced me as a writer who was now living in New York and had mentioned that I was currently working on a feminist book. The man asked me what exactly my book was about. I didn't get to say much. I began with "I'm chronicling one hundred instances of blatant sexism I've experienced, including discrimination, assault, and . . ."

He cut me off. "Yeah, but sexism goes both ways." He laughed and swigged his beer. I was happy not to be so young anymore in that moment. When I was younger, I used to become intimidated by the sheer force of the confidence of the men around me. There's an air many straight men have in the rural area where I'm from, especially when they're talking to women, a dismissive, jocular confidence. The way this man interrupted me and jovially dismissed the entire premise of my book signaled to me that he was used to bulldozing women into agreeing with his opinions. I think he expected me to say, "Oh, well sure, sexism goes both ways, but it's worse for women." Then he could tell me that, "the grass is always greener on the other side." Then we could laugh like we were in it together; as if there is an inherent bond between men and women that requires a certain level of dissonance and disenfranchisement to be maintained.

Luckily, I am older and surer of myself. I said, "No it doesn't. Sexism doesn't go both ways. That's not even possible."

His eyebrows furrowed and he looked confused. "You're telling me women never treat men badly too?"

"No, that's not what I mean at all. That's not what sexism is. You're not systematically oppressed *because* you're a man. You're not discriminated against *because* you're a man. You're not disproportionately in danger of being harassed, raped, and killed *because* you're a man."

I have a lot of statistics in my head. I have memorized only the most heavily researched statistics on the impact of sexism that have been corroborated by numerous reports and studies from the Department of Justice, the CDC, the FBI, and university research departments and private institutions. These statistics are verifiable across the board in multiple studies. When trying to explain to men that sexism does not, in fact, go both ways, that there is no equivalent, I often pull these out: One in three women have been raped, while one in seventy-one men have been raped. Ninety-nine percent of rapes are committed by men, ninety-seven percent of all violent crime is committed by men, and the number one killer of women worldwide between the ages of fifteen and fifty is male violence. Women are still paid sixty-five cents for every dollar men make, and the disparity is even greater for women of color.

But I didn't say any of these statistics, because there is one statistic that actually seems to impact men enough to make them actually think about what I'm saying; that there is no equivalent. Women aren't doing this to men. I said, "Do you know what the number one cause of death is for pregnant women in the US?"

He nodded, "Yeah, yeah, I know. Murder by their male partners."

This was a fairly new statistic that had come out in the past year. Previously, when collecting data on mortality rates among pregnant women, causes of death directly related to complications with the pregnancy were taken into consideration. But a number of studies that looked at causes of death for pregnant women, including those not related to health complications, found that the number one cause of death of women who are pregnant is male violence. When I first read this, I was sickened and struck with disbelief. I assumed this would be anyone's reaction.

"Okay, so you know." I said. "Well, there it is. There's no equivalent. Pregnant women aren't murdering their male partners at epidemic rates that actually qualify as a major health risk."

"Yeah, that's bad," he said, "but," and then he said something truly revealing. He said, "You gotta think, what was her part in that? When that happens, you know, when a pregnant woman is murdered by her partner, that's a relationship. There are two sides to that. And you have to think, what did she do leading up to that to push the guy to go that far?"

The three other men standing with us nodded in agreement.

"Right?" one of them said.

"I don't think I'm better than women. I'm a misogynist. I *hate* women." And then he laughed. "You know what I'm saying though."

"No, I actually don't," I said.

"That's why men hate women," he told me. "Because honestly, you have more power over us than we have over you and you know it."

I realized he thought we were locked in some age-old battle of the sexes, and I was the feisty woman who he had to win over. Not a person who was responding to something extremely bigoted, which was about me, spoken by a person who held a position of social power over me. He didn't see sexism as bigotry. He saw it as a natural order. So many men do. So many men, when I talk about systematic sexism, bring it back down to the one-on-one, the interpersonal interactions they have with individual women. When we talk about epidemic levels of violence against women, even epidemic levels of murder, they talk about a girlfriend who smacked them. When I talk about the pay gap between men and women, they talk about the pressure put on men to be the breadwinners in a marriage. It's all reflexive. They don't think of women as people who exist outside of their relationship to men.

98

I was thirty-six, attending a comedy show in Brooklyn with a male friend of mine, Joseph. We were getting ready to leave, and Joseph went to the restroom. I waited for him at the bar. There weren't many other people. It was a quiet night. I opened my bag and rummaged around, looking for my ChapStick, and a man sitting catty-corner to me at the bar said, "You scared?"

I zipped my bag shut and looked at him. He was a homely man, around my age, and he was leaning forward, sneering at me like a cartoon villain. "What?" I said, not understanding.

He rested his arm on the bar and leaned toward me, "You scared?" he asked again.

"No," I said.

"You're not scared," he said. "You look scared."

"What?" I said. This was bizarre.

"Maybe you should be scared. You scared? You scarrrr . . ." He trailed off, mumbling the end of the word, as he glanced up over my shoulder. Joseph had come back and was standing right next to me, staring at this man with a look that said, 'What the hell are you doing?' like he'd just caught a child doing something ridiculously wrong. The man sat back in his chair and waved his hand. "Uh, maybe I shouldn't have said that," he grumbled, glancing from me to Joseph, nervously.

Later, Joseph said it was like the man had "run out of batteries" when he saw a man with me. He'd stood back and watched our interaction for a few minutes before he approached. "You were just standing there," he said, "not doing anything, and he was like, heckling you while you were performing some menial task, just looking through your bag. Then, when I came up and stood next to you he thought, 'Oh no, I don't get to play this weird, misogynist game anymore, because there's a supervisor in the room.'"

I was glad Joseph had seen it, because this almost never happens when I am out in public with a male friend and that's why our experiences as women are so often invisible to the men who would find this behavior abhorrent.

99

I was thirty-six, sitting in a Seattle pizza restaurant
that also has a bar. I often frequent this place for a drink and
a pizza at happy hour. I was eating and waiting for my girlfriend and her daughter to join me. I had about forty minutes
to kill before they got there. I ordered a drink and the man
sitting at the bar next to me struck up a conversation with me.
We chatted about the current political situation, and about
his recently moving to the neighborhood, Capitol Hill. He
told me about his wife and kids, and the new house he'd just
purchased, and how much his family loved it. This seemed to
me to be a friendly conversation. After about thirty minutes of
sporadic chatting, he told me he was going to sit on the patio
of the restaurant and have a cigarette and asked if I would like
to join him. I did. We sat outside at a table smoking, and he
came on to me. He asked me if I'd like to go back to his house
with him. I deflected, saying, "I don't think your wife would
like that." He told me his wife was out of town on vacation,
complimented my looks, and asked again. This time I was
firmer. I said, "My partner and her daughter are coming here
in a few minutes. I'm in a relationship. I just wanted this to be
a friendly conversation, okay?"

He smiled at me and leaned in. Then he said, "I like
you, I can tell you like me. Come on." Then he grabbed my

breast and squeezed it. I smacked his hand away, stood up, and began yelling at him. I was in the process of writing this book when this happened and something about the fact that I'd been writing about sexual assault every day for months made this particular groping incident more potent for me. I'd been analyzing all of my different stages of interacting with men throughout my life that led up to assault and harassment. With this man, I'd been firm and unequivocally clear about my lack of interest in having sex with him and it had still happened. Was the only option to not speak to men I don't know? I didn't want to live in that world.

I angrily asked him, "Why did you do that? Why did you think it was okay?"

He responded by saying, "Oh, you liked it a little?"

"No, I didn't!" I told him heatedly. "You just grabbed my breasts! I told you I didn't want to fuck you, and so you just grabbed my fucking breast. *Why?*"

He threw his hands in the air and shouted back aggressively, "What do you want from me? You want all my money? You want to destroy my family? You want to take my life?" Then he got up and left in a huff.

I didn't go back to the restaurant for months. When I did go back, it was with my partner. After we sat down and ordered our drinks and pizza at the bar, this same man came in and sat at the end of the bar. He didn't notice me at first, and began talking to a woman next to him. After about ten minutes, he got handsy with her, putting his arm around her and being obviously flirtatious. It was hard to tell if she minded or if she knew him, but I was glad he hadn't noticed me or if he had, was ignoring me. I didn't really want to be anywhere near him, so when our food came, my girlfriend and I decided to move out to the patio. When I stood up, he saw me from the end of the bar, and he stood and yelled at the bartender to get me a shot on him. I walked away and as I exited, he tried to get my attention, flirtatiously yelling at me to have a drink with him. I made eye contact and shook my head no, pointedly. "Are you fucking kidding me?" I mumbled.

A couple hours later, I went in to pay my bill and he was no longer there. I decided to tell the bartender what had happened and why I hadn't come in for a few months. I told him that the man who'd tried to order a shot for me, which the bartender had noticed (and had found his interaction with me odd), had come on to me and when I rejected his advances, had grabbed my breasts.

The bartender's face turned red with anger. "Oh, he's fucking done!" he shouted. "You're the *third* woman who's complained about him this month!" He shook his head. "You will *not* see him in here again. Don't worry. You're not the only woman he's had a problem with. He's fucking *done!*" Then he went and informed the bouncer the man wasn't to be allowed in the bar ever again.

100

This also happened while I was writing this book. Because of a technical error, my account name on Lyft is John Smith and I'm not able to change this without deleting my account and setting the whole thing up again, so out of sheer laziness, I never have.

I was in Brooklyn. A Lyft driver picked me up and when I got into the car he asked, "Are you John?"

I said, "Yes, that's the name on my account."

He said, "Your name is John?"

I said, "No. It's just a glitch. I can't fix it without deleting my entire account."

He laughed and said, "Oh, because you are much sexier than a John, you know? This was a pleasant surprise. You are sexy. I don't expect a John to be sexy."

At this point, he was driving. I was alone in a moving car with this man I don't know and when cabdrivers are inappropriate with me, I don't feel complimented. I feel afraid.

For the record, most Lyft drivers in New York City are also certified city cabs. This man drove a black cab with an NYC medallion and also used Lyft and Uber, which means he has had some formal training as a cabdriver.

The driver continued eyeing me in the rearview mirror. "Why don't you tell people it's your boyfriend's account?"

he asked. I shook my head no. "Do you have a boy-friend?"

"Nope," I grunted.

"No boyfriend? Why not?" He asked me. "You're sexy."

I usually don't do this in cabs or with straight men I don't know, because I'm often worried they might be homophobic enough to actually kill me. But at this point, I was in a Lyft, which has my info and his, and I was annoyed, so I squared my shoulders and said in a deep, assertive voice, "I don't have a boyfriend because I'm a lesbian," hoping to shut him down.

This made him pause. He was totally silent for five seconds, thinking deeply, then he said, "Oh yeah? I had a gay guy in my car a few nights ago. I was driving this gay guy around, and . . ." He went on to tell me how this gay man had hit on him, but, "I'm not like that. I'm not gay. The guy had the wrong idea." Then he made a disgusted noise and laughed, then he looked in the mirror at me again and said, "You're hot."

I nodded, "Okay."

"Your name's not John, though?"

"Nope."

"What's your real name?"

"Chavisa," I told him. In these situations, I power through and try to avoid conflict that might end up in violence against me, until I can get out and get away. I've found men like this, who are unable to understand obvious hints that I'm not interested, don't get angry or violent if they still think they have any chance at flirting. And he still did seem to think this, although I'd shown him no interest and clearly said I was a dyke. It's a weird catch-22 most women understand. If men aren't able to comprehend a clear "no," then they are probably scary enough that it's easier to acquiesce until you can get away. So, I told him my first name.

He started repeating my name incorrectly, saying it was unique, asking where it's from. "My mom made it up."

Then he said several times, "Shabissa, shabissa, that's such a sexy name. So hot! That name is just *hot*. You know how some names are just hot names, right? That's hot. Don't you think some names are just hot?" He stared at me as if for an answer.

I said, "No. I don't know."

He said, "Yeah, for sure! Don't you think some names just say '*sex*'? Your name does. You are sexy, and your name is sexy."

"What *other* names?" I said dryly.

He paused and thought about it, then he said, "*Pussy!*"

(I fucking kid you not. He shouted, "*Pussy!*")

Yep.

There was a long pause. I didn't respond. Then he said again, "Yeah, *Pussy!*"

I thought it was best not to say anything else, since he was now shouting "pussy!" at me under the guise of it being a hot name, which, of course, well . . . "pussy" is not even a *name*.

After I didn't respond in any way to him saying "pussy" repeatedly, but stared tensely at the seat-back, he offered, "And Catalina? That's a hot name? Hey, *what do you think*? Catalina?" Long pause. "Michelle?"

"Those are names," I said.

"Nice, right?" He said. "*Hot* names?"

I nodded. Then he spent a full minute nervously saying every female name that came into his head, just listing them . . . "Sarah, Emily, Tanya, flower names? Liliana?"

Then we got to my stop and he tried to give me his number, for a business he was starting up selling women's underwear that I might like to buy. I tried to open the door and get out, but it was locked and he wasn't unlocking it, even though he could see me clearly trying to open my door.

He handed me his phone and showed me pictures of women's Egyptian cotton underwear that he said he was going to be selling for an online business next month. He insisted I take his number. So I got out my phone and texted his number to my girlfriend in a message that said, "This cabdriver is scaring me. This is his personal number."

He told me to text him so he would have my number too. I told him that I wrote his number down and that I would contact him about the underwear. Then he unlocked the doors and told me to have a lovely night and to please leave him five stars on Lyft, smiling and waving as he said goodbye, as if this had been a pleasant time for both of us.

I left him no tip and one star and immediately reported him to Lyft.

That ride still cost me eight dollars.

Pussy is not a name.

acknowledgments

I must extend my deepest gratitude and enduring love to my partner, Bekka Sartwell, for her patience with, and care for me as I wrote this emotionally turbulent book.

I would also like to thank David Murray for his generous support and friendship.

Thanks to my editor, Sanina Clark, for being there with me every step of the way as I completed this manuscript.

Finally, I would like to send my gratitude back in time, to my twenty-one-year-old self, for choosing to stay alive so that I could grow into a place where I feel empowered enough to speak clearly and openly about the things that seemed so impossible to survive.

About the Author

Brooklyn-based writer CHAVISA WOODS is the author of the short story collection *Things to Do When You're Goth in the Country* (Seven Stories Press, 2017), about which *Booklist*, in a starred review, wrote, "This book is tight, intelligent, and important, and sure to secure Woods a seat in the pantheon of critical 21st century voices;" the novel *The Albino Album* (Seven Stories Press, 2013); and the story collection *Love Does Not Make Me Gentle or Kind* (Fly by Night Press, 2009). She was the recipient of the 2014 Cobalt Prize for fiction and was a finalist in 2009, 2014, and 2018 for the Lambda Literary Award for fiction. In 2018 she was the recipient of the Kathy Acker Award for Writing and the Shirley Jackson Award for Best Novelette. Woods has appeared as a featured author at such notable venues as the Whitney Museum of American Art, City Lights Bookstore, Town Hall Seattle, the Brecht Forum, the Cervantes Institute, and St. Mark's Poetry Project.

About the Publisher

SEVEN STORIES PRESS is an independent book publisher based in New York City. We publish works of the imagination by such writers as Nelson Algren, Russell Banks, Octavia E. Butler, Ani DiFranco, Assia Djebar, Ariel Dorfman, Coco Fusco, Barry Gifford, Martha Long, Luis Negrón, Peter Plate, Hwang Sok-yong, Lee Stringer, and Kurt Vonnegut, to name a few, together with political titles by voices of conscience, including Subhankar Banerjee, the Boston Women's Health Collective, Noam Chomsky, Angela Y. Davis, Human Rights Watch, Derrick Jensen, Ralph Nader, Loretta Napoleoni, Gary Null, Greg Palast, Project Censored, Barbara Seaman, Alice Walker, Gary Webb, and Howard Zinn, among many others. Seven Stories Press believes publishers have a special responsibility to defend free speech and human rights, and to celebrate the gifts of the human imagination, wherever we can. In 2012 we launched Triangle Square books for young readers with strong social justice and narrative components, telling personal stories of courage and commitment. For additional information, visit www.sevenstories.com.